Purrs of Praise!

Heart-touching and insightful, reading *Purr Prints of the Heart* is like being wrapped up in a warm hug of comfort. Deborah Barnes and Mr. Jazz show us that the spiritual connection with our departed cats never dies."

~**Ingrid King**, award-winning author of *Buckley's Story: Lessons from a Feline Master Teacher*, and publisher of *The Conscious Cat*

"Deborah Barnes exhibits her writing prowess as she bears her soul in the poignant memoir, *Purr Prints of the Heart*, brilliantly narrated by the book's muse, "Mr. Jazz." Reader's emotions will be stirred to their core as Barnes magnificently climbs into the mind, heart and soul of not only Mr. Jazz, but cats as a whole and the humans who devote their lives to them. *Purr Prints* takes the reader on a journey that is like a salve in book form that offers comfort to all who have had to deal with (or will have to deal with), the inevitable loss of a beloved pet. Written with eloquence, grace, humor and a love that transcends the pages, I defy any pet lover not to see themselves depicted in this literary treasure."

~**Caren Gittleman**, publisher of *Cat Chat with Caren and Cody*

"*Purr Prints of the Heart* is a touching tale of beginnings, endings and the beauty of life. Deborah and Jazz beautifully remind us that our time with loved ones is precious, but even death can't separate hearts."

~**Angie Bailey**, author of *Texts from Mittens* and *Whiskerslist: The Kitty Classifieds*

"Deborah Barnes has created a supportive gift with a book that soothes the broken hearts of bereaved pet lovers of all ages as her cat, Jazz, unfolds the story of his life and end of life with her. Readers enjoy the quirks of pets living in multiple pet households with other cats and dogs. We are all enriched by Barnes who gives us a psycho-emotional glimpse into the wonders of the human-animal bond and the natural feelings of grief and denial during end of life decision making and the difficult days of pet loss."
    ~**Alice Villalobos**, DVM, FNAP / *www.pawspice.com*

"*Purr Prints of the Heart* will touch your soul. If you are not already a pet lover, you will be after reading this insightful and inspirational book."
    ~**Robert Hudson**, host and founder, *Pet Radio Show.com*

"Bravo! A beautiful story of life, love and lessons. *Purr Prints of the Heart* is a touching memoir of Mr. Jazz, a cat who shares his unique perspective on the conversation of pet loss to help human's better cope when losing a beloved family pet."
    ~**Charmaine Hammond**, best-selling author & professional speaker

"Anyone who has ever lost a beloved pet will find comfort reading Deborah Barnes' poignant book, *Purr Prints of the Heart*. This extraordinary story takes us through the journey of Ragdoll kitty, Mr. Jazz, in his very own wise and loving voice. You will take the steps to your own healing and emotional recovery when you laugh with Mr. Jazz as he shares his kitten antics while growing up, and cry with him as he bravely faces his crossover to the Rainbow Bridge. Complete with a practical guide for coping with pet loss, *Purr Prints of the Heart* is a touching celebration of life and the beautiful bond we share with our pets."
    ~**Susan Logan-McCracken,** co-author of *Cat Calls* and longtime editor of *Cat Fancy* magazine

"Written from the omniscient view of her cat Mr. Jazz, author Deb Barnes masterfully enlightens readers about cat behavior and how they communicate with humans and other pets through stages of life, love, and loss. Replete with memorable moments of anticipation, outbursts of laughter, sighs of relief, sheer joy, and throes of grief, this book is cleverly written in cat likeness with steady prose, candor, grace, and humor. More importantly, it offers readers unique guidance on coping with the loss of a beloved pet. The ending is a welcoming upturn, a refreshing reminder of the celebration of life and the indelible purr prints cats leave on our hearts."

~**Christine Michaels**, founder and president of *Pawsitively Humane*

"*Purr Prints of the Heart* reaches across to all of us with lessons in compassion, kindness, and discovery. After reading the story through the voice of Mr. Jazz, you will no longer look at the cats you share your life with and wonder what they are thinking... about you, about life and, especially, about love and letting go. Four paws up for Deb Barnes!! You've reached out and touched this heart of mine!!"

~**Bonnie Poirier**, pastor at Ministry of St. Francis of Assisi

"Our animal companions have many lessons to teach us humans, and they know the most difficult one for us is to recognize, understand and accept when they tell us they are ready to leave this life. Deb's deft characterization of Mr. Jazz's quiet personality and gentle humor carries us in his own voice from his mother's first lessons through 15 years to his final transition from body to spirit and afterward as we watch him mature into this understanding and wordlessly share it with his human family."

~**Bernadette E. Kazmarski**, award-winning artist and writer, publisher of *The Creative Cat*

PURR PRINTS
OF THE HEART

A Cat's Tale of Life, Death, and Beyond

Deborah Barnes

as told by Mr. Jazz the Cat

Rachel —
In tribute to all
the animals that
have a spot in your heart.
Purrs —
Deb Barnes

ZZP PUBLISHING LLC

Purr Prints of the Heart

ZZP PUBLISHING, LLC
PO Box 770625
Coral Springs, FL 33077
www.zzppublishing.com

Printed in the USA
Charleston, SC

Acknowledgements
Book Cover and Interior Design: Deborah Barnes
Photos: Dan Power
Editing: Karen Robinson
Associate Editing: Pamela Bushnell

First Edition: April 2015

Library of Congress Control Number: 2015902684

ISBN 978-0-9834408-1-9

*In loving memory of those cherished
pets we have lost but not forgotten...*

Foreword

I TAKE FULL CREDIT for this book. And if Deb Barnes saw a show on Animal Planet, featuring Ragdolls that motivated her to get one that ultimately wound up writing his *Purr Prints of the Heart* meow memoir, then I was one of the experts on the show talking about the breed. Still, as much as I'd like to think this book is all about me, alas it's not.

When Jazz lands his new home as a kitten, he finds he is sharing it with other cats and dogs – all with their own individual personas. Barnes deftly reminds us throughout the story that just as we are all unique individuals, molded by our genetics and our experiences, the same is true for cats, and for that matter, dogs.

I love it when authors bust feline fallacies. Most cat guardians live with just over two cats on average. In this story several cats live peaceably. However, many believe that cats are solitary creatures. Untrue. Of course, the problem is that most people who don't know better are unaware because they've never been privileged enough to share their life with cats.

Cats find their way into our homes all sorts of ways, including rescue organizations or cats we rescue from the streets. According to this book, and the cats that "speak" in it, they do appreciate that we've given them a better life. I'm not sure that cats truly cognitively think this. But like most of us, I'd like to think so.

Over time characters come and go in the story – both humans and animals. But being introduced to them and getting to feel you know them doesn't stop the cycle of life as Barnes poignantly shares – from the tragic loss of her beloved *Golden Retriever Bailey at the far too young age of two to cancer, to opening her heart again to recent adoptions, rescue kittens Kizmet and Jazmine, Barnes learns from the wise Mr. Jazz that we can always love again after loss.

One thing that never changes is change itself. Of course, cats are slow to accept change, and at times Mr. Jazz is particularly resistant. Clearly, Barnes loved and loves her purr-family. But like so many suggest because we increasingly love our pets with all our hearts, it's progressively difficult to let go. But there always comes a time. And perhaps as Mr. Jazz would lead us to believe, our pets know it, even if we don't and they let us know when it is time to let them go. Sad yes, very sad, but life goes on. And soon there will be another kitten, puppy or rescued pet to love and be loved.

~**Steve Dale**, CABC (Certified Animal Behavior Consultant); syndicated newspaper columnist (Tribune Content Agency) and syndicated radio host (Black Dog Radio Productions). Among his books is *Good Cat*; he's a contributor to many books including *The Cat: Clinical Medicine and Management* (edited by Dr. Susan Little). He's a contributor to *Behavior Guidelines for Indoor Cats* (American Association of Feline Practitioners) and is the primary author of CATegorical Care (American Humane Association/CATaylst Council). Steve is a longtime Board member of the Winn Feline Foundation and Tree House Humane Society (Chicago). He is a founder of the CATalyst Council, and past Board member. He's the recipient of many awards, including the AVMA Humane Award.

*Sadly, it's true; an apparent significant subset of the Golden Retriever breed is that they are succumbing to cancer far too early in life. This is why the Morris Animal Foundation has enlisted about 2,500 dogs in the Golden Retriever Lifetime study. This epic study is the first of its kind in veterinary medicine (learn more at www.morrisanimalfoundation.org)

Contents

Prologue

MY NAME IS MR. JAZZ. I'm a Ragdoll cat and on August 28, 2013, after 15 years of life, I asked my beloved humans for the most difficult gift of all – to help me cross the Rainbow Bridge. I'd never asked them for much of anything else before that – I was always a humble cat with simple desires – quiet naps on the couch, the love of my family, and a full belly were all I really cared about, and those needs were always fulfilled. I never aspired toward fame, and writing my story wasn't part of my master plan.

But the truth is my death deeply touched the hearts of a wide audience and I couldn't ignore that there appeared to be a greater purpose to it all – my death brought with it lessons learned that need to be told from my point of view so anyone who has ever loved and had to say goodbye to a cherished pet can understand from a pet's perspective that when it's our time to go, we want you to let us, no matter how difficult that might be for you. We want you to understand when that moment happens and we are gone from your life in the physical sense, we remain in your hearts and souls forevermore and the intense pain you feel as you grieve will eventually soften, to be replaced with the memories of happier days shared with us.

Naturally, I realize parts of this story will undoubtedly sadden some of you – after all it's about my death – but that's not my intention at all, and I hope it won't stop you from reading on. This story is really a celebration. A celebration of my life and the life of all animals that find a way into the hearts and homes of our human guardians across the world, whatever our unique circumstances might be. We're grateful for the love, companionship, and care you give us, for however long or brief that moment on this earth may be and my story is about honoring that relationship and being able to find the joy, beauty, and dignity of letting us go when it's our time.

Talking about my death does require a look back into my life, and when I think about how it all began for me, the first thing I can recall with any clarity is the minute-by-minute battle I shared with several other squirming beings that looked just like me to find the warm milk of our mother. I couldn't tell you how many of us there were as I was unable to count at that young stage of my life, but I do remember my mother as a strong and stunning cat who kept us warm, fed, and clean. I honestly don't remember much else because most of my life at this point centered on living with her in the tiny room I shared with her and my siblings.

Besides my mother, two big creatures took care of us. They weren't of the feline persuasion and were my first introduction to what was apparently the human species. They were an oddity for sure – they had no hind legs and very little fur – and I remember they towered over us like giants on two upright front legs they were able to balance on without falling over. They also had funny paws that looked like long, scary claws and rather than meowing softly to communicate like my mother did with us, they spoke in loud, booming voices.

One of them was a male, the other was a female, and instead of smelling comforting like our mother did – an intoxicating perfume of milk and cat kibble – they smelled of things I couldn't discern yet – things my mother likened to sweat, coffee, and wet dog. I can't say they were necessarily mean to us, but they weren't overly friendly either, and one of the things I do recall them saying was that our mother had a pedigree, which apparently gave them the liberty to constantly let other big humans barge into our not-so-private room.

These other humans would stare and point at us, and sometimes they would reach in to pick up one of us from our mother without her permission to hold us with their monster paws. We would softly mew in startled protest for them to put us back down, but they would laugh at us, telling us how cute our little meows sounded as they kissed our faces! They referred to our mother as a Queen, and one day I overheard one of them say to another that the reason they came to see us was because they planned on taking us, one by one, from our mother to a new home!

Even though my memory of days gone by might be hazy at times, I can assure you *that* was a moment forever etched in my mind! I was instantly awash with panic, and my little kitten head filled with a barrage of questions that all jumbled together into one plaintive wail. A lot of humans had been coming by. Who were they going to take and why? Would we all be going to the same home? Was someone going to take me? Why couldn't we all stay together with our mother? I remember trying to calm myself, but it was so confusing. And why would our mother let us go? Certainly if she were a Queen, she would have special rights and privileges. Why wouldn't she scratch and fight and hiss to keep us all together with her? I just didn't understand any of it. Were we bad kitties being punished for something? And then one day my mother took me to the side and explained it all.

Apparently the human caretakers used her beautiful markings and lineage (she was a stunning Chocolate Point Bicolor Ragdoll) to make more kitties like her because other humans wanted us as their own pet-children. These humans paid money, whatever that was, to the caretakers for us. She explained that being chosen by one of these humans was actually a big honor – these humans had kind and loving hearts and I should look forward to going home with one of them. When she explained it to me like that, it started to make a little more sense, but I could tell deep down she knew I was still scared and confused and she was worried about me.

I mewed back to her with hesitant conviction that I understood what she was telling me. My mother was so beautiful, patient, and knowledgeable. I wanted more than anything to make her happy and proud of me, so in between my predictable kitten stages of growth – learning to walk on my wobbly legs, wrestling nonstop with my brothers and sisters, learning how to eat solid foods, and becoming litter box trained – I dreamed day and night of finding my own human to adopt me.

What I didn't realize at the time was that my mother really wanted me safe too and that was why she was so worried. For you see, despite her kind and gentle disposition and her glorious silky fur coat and impeccable credentials, the house we lived in was not in the best condition and was hardly a place a mother cat would aspire for her children to grow up in. She had already resigned herself to her lot in life, but she wanted better for us.

Since I had lived all of my matter of weeks of life in the warm and loving comfort of my mother and my siblings and I had never ventured out of the four walls of our tiny room, I didn't know any better and didn't notice all the acrid smells around me. Apparently the house we lived in was inhabited by other Ragdoll cats of various sizes, sexes, and ages, climbing all over the counters and furniture, and there was also a resident dog. The numerous litter boxes scattered about the house were in need of a good cleaning and the human caretakers never let the dog outside for bathroom privileges. Instead, they would put newspaper on the floor in the kitchen for the dog to use, so you can only imagine what the house smelled like.

Probably as a result of all this, I had a cough and an eye infection. My mother didn't have the heart to tell me this, but that was why she was worried. Who would want to adopt a sick kitten, let alone one they had to pay for? But because she was a cat of such grace and class, making the surroundings beautiful by her presence, I never sensed her fears and didn't know any better. She was certain in her heart that one day the perfect human would come and rescue me, despite my medical maladies, because she believed me to be a very special cat. Perhaps she hadn't quite known I would become an author one day, but she always knew from the very beginning I was destined for greater things, and she insisted I was a cat with a message to share and lessons to teach.

So in my mother's mind, it couldn't be just any someone and she didn't want to rush things. She always told me she would know in her heart when it would be the right human, and each time someone came and picked out one of my brothers or sisters, overlooking me, she told me to be patient. She never let on that I was different, and her only wish was that her beloved baby boy find a warm, safe, clean, and loving home.

"My handsome, darling boy," she would say to me. "No ordinary human will do – the human who picks you will understand you have something special that not all cats have. You have a rare gift – even though you're still young, you were born with an old soul heart. Not all cats are bestowed with this blessing, and it gives you a unique kindness, wisdom, and compassion that only an equally special human will recognize, appreciate, and understand. Once you meet this human, you will forevermore have an irrevocable bond that will transcend the likes of this world and beyond."

She would nuzzle my head and purr and somehow I just knew she was right. I didn't understand all of her big and fancy words, but her loving tone was clear – I was a special cat destined for a special life.

She Picked Me

SOMETHING WAS DIFFERENT about this one. She still had funny paws and didn't have fur, other than what was sprouting from her head, but she was tinier than most of the others who came to look at us and spoke with a soft and kind voice. And rather than scoop one of us up without warning like some of the others did, she sat on the floor next to our mother, gently petting her, and asked for permission to hold one of us!

But even more unbelievably, this polite being who wanted to hold one of us was looking at me! I held my breath and dared not blink, lest I was imagining things, but I saw her reach toward me.

"Hey," said the female human caretaker. "That one's sick. Don't even bother picking him up. We're giving him medicine, but you won't want him. Look at one of the other kittens – they're so much more beautiful than him, and they're healthy."

Sick? Not beautiful? What was the female caretaker talking about? My mother told me all the time I was the most handsome kitten in the whole world and somebody would want me because I was special. I was raised from the moment I could understand that my one and only job in life was to have one of those furless, pawless creatures fall in love with me so they would pick me to come live with them in what my mother referred to as my "furever home."

The thought that nobody would want me never entered my mind as I saw myself through the eyes of my brothers and sisters who were perfectly formed, healthy, creamy balls of silky fur with beautiful clear blue eyes. I felt the tears well up in my cloudy eyes and I had a lump in my throat.

I had let my mother down. Something was wrong with me and I would never find my special furever home. Why was I different? It wasn't fair. I was a good boy who never caused any trouble – it was always my other siblings that started our wrestling matches and tracked their dirty paw prints all over the floor from stepping in our food dishes. I was devastated to know that behind my back I was considered a misfit no one would ever want.

But with a very clear and strong voice, the tiny human said, "I *do* want that one. He's absolutely perfect just the way he is, and I think he's the most beautiful kitten I've ever seen. When can I bring him home?"

Home? She said *home*! I didn't hear the word "furever," but I could tell from the tone of her voice it was implied, and if I had been allowed to roam to the top of the roof, I would have meowed with joy for the whole world to hear. "Hey everybody, she picked me! Someone does want me! Someone does care and I *am* special!"

She saw past the gunk running down my left eye, staining the white of my fur to a brownish color, and she didn't even wince when I sneezed a series of wet hellos right into her face. She just kissed the top of my head and caressed my baby fur, causing my motor to run like it did when I kneaded my paws into the soft belly of my mother. She whispered to me that she had nursed many a kitty back to health in her day and that she would always love me for who I was on the inside, not what I looked like on the outside.

Eventually she put me back down next to my mother so she could talk to the female caretaker. I heard bits and pieces of the conversation. According to my mother, these talking humans came in all kinds of shapes, sizes, personalities, and colors just like cats did. The kind-hearted human who wanted me was a female, and she also brought a couple of other humans with her who were smaller than her. They were males like me, and they called her "Mom." I guess collectively they made up what was called a family, and my mother said that was even better news for me – having one human love me was incredible, but having a whole family was amazing according to her!

Even though I was excited and extremely proud of myself for finally being chosen, I couldn't go with the female human and her offspring right away because I was still too young to leave my mother. Apparently it's best if kittens are at least 10 weeks old before they leave the nest – that way they are fully weaned and it makes the transition much safer and healthier for the kitten. So even though it tore at her heart to leave me, she wanted what was best for me and agreed to come back in a couple of weeks when I would be old enough to leave my mother.

I never questioned her loyalty. I knew she would be back for me, and even though I would never tell this to her directly and risk hurting her feelings, I was kind of glad I didn't have to go with her right away because deep down I was scared to leave my mother and my siblings. My life wasn't perfect, but it was the life I was used to and I wasn't as brave as I let on. I was relieved to have some time to talk with my mother to share my fears and excitement with her and to tell her how much I loved her and that I would never forget her.

We spent every moment together, and on those occasions when I wasn't napping, she never tired of telling me what my new life would be like. "Darling boy," she would purr. "You will have a wonderful life. Your new family will love you with all of their hearts and will make sure you have a life filled with sunbeams, warm and cozy laps, delicious treats, clean litter, nutritious food, fun toys, and lots and lots of love."

"You will love them back in return," she continued. "But you will also have to teach them because, while they mean well, these humans without fur and with funny paws are not as wise as you'll grow up to be one day and they'll need to learn from you. They can be especially impatient creatures and often forget to take the time to appreciate the simple beauty of life around them, like napping in a sunbeam or chasing a moth."

She went on. "As a pet to a family of humans, the physical time you spend with them will be limited in the collective span of their lives and you will have to remind them to make each and every day they share with you special because even though you can't imagine it now, time will pass in a heartbeat, and the next thing you know, your time on this earth will have to come to an end with them and they'll have to say goodbye to you. This will make them very sad and often they don't know how to let go – it will be up to you to be patient and show them the way when it's time. I know it might sound scary right now, but I promise you it's not. You'll be ready when the time is right. Until then, enjoy each and every moment with them and be the best cat you can be. All will be right in your world, I promise you that."

I wasn't too sure about what she had told me – quite frankly it seemed like an awful lot of responsibility to me, and I wasn't sure if I was up to the challenge. Wise? I was still a kitten and my days consisted of napping, eating, and playing. I didn't know how much more I could offer outside of that. I assumed by having a new furever home I would just be expected to be a sweet, loyal, and charming pet that napped, ate, and played. I already had all that cornered. All this talk of life, death, and teaching lessons was daunting, but not wanting to disappoint my mother, I just purred my love and agreement and went to bed in anticipation of the morning when my new life would begin.

My New Home

SLEEPING A RESTLESS, Christmas Eve kind of night, morning finally arrived and after a tearful goodbye to my mother, it was time for the tiny female human to bring me to my new furever home, but I already had to question my mother's logic. Was this really what she'd imagined for me? This was supposed to be my destiny, so what did I do to deserve such cruel punishment?

Where was the love? The toys? The sunbeams and warm laps to nap on? Had the tiny human tricked my mother with her kindness? The indignity of it all – one minute the human was nuzzling my neck and crooning her love to me, whispering that I'm going to my new home and then the next I was jammed into a tiny jail with little air holes and metal bars on the door. What was going on? Was this meant to be my new home? What kind of nonsense was this? Sure, the female human was sitting next to me, soothing me with kind words, but why did I feel like the ground was moving, and where was I going?

I don't know how much time passed – my little lungs were so tired from screaming to be set free from my prison that I didn't realize the movement had stopped and the tiny human had lifted me from the moving machine to take me to yet another cruel punishment that I didn't deserve. I tentatively peered from the holes in my cage to see I was in a room that had a vaguely familiar smell to me – one of rubbing alcohol and disinfectants. I recognized it from the times the female caretaker took my siblings and me to have a needle stuck in us for something called vaccinations at a place she called the "Vets Office." What is up with humans? Why the prisons, needles, and moving machines? I again flashed back to tales of sunbeams, treats, and toys. Lies, lies, and more lies.

Well, regardless, this certainly couldn't be good news, so I settled myself as close to the back of the cage as I could, hoping I'd made myself invisible to these conniving humans, and I closed my eyes to think of my mother. Surely she knew what she was talking about when she told me about the happiness I would find living with my furever family. I knew she loved me and would never deliberately lead me down a path filled with nothing but torment and torture. I could hear her in my mind.

"Be patient, little one," she said to me. "If your human is doing something you don't understand right now, I promise you there's a reason for it and everything will turn out okay. You'll see." I hoped she was right, but my thoughts were rudely interrupted as I was snatched out of my prison by the tiny female human, aka the traitor, and plopped onto a table that was cold and hard to my skin.

Oh boy, I silently thought to my mother. This was really testing my patience, and just when I thought things couldn't possibly get any worse, a big male human wearing a white coat with pockets came into the room and, without any warning or fanfare, other than telling me how adorable I was, assaulted me by shoving a strange apparatus down my ears! He went by the name "Vet," and I thought my heart was going to burst from my chest; it was beating so fast from his shenanigans. Like it was the most natural thing in the world, he moved on to shine a light into my eyes, and then he poked my butt with a thermometer to take my temperature!

Oh, my stars – the humiliation of it all. But honestly, despite the bodily invasion, I can't say the vet human was being unjustly mean to me – I sensed he had a kind heart – but the poking and prodding just added to the indignity of an already long, confusing, and stressful day, and I just wanted to go home. Whatever that meant. Willing myself not to cry, my thoughts were interrupted again, this time by his voice.

"Well," he said to the tiny female human. "Good thing you brought him in for a checkup before you went home. Just like you thought – this little guy still has a lingering infection and needs to be put into quarantine before you can introduce him to the rest of the cats in your house. He'll need drops in his eyes three times a day and an antibiotic for his cough."

Antibiotic? Quarantine? And I was contagious? Heaven help me, but what did all of that mean? All of those words were new to me, and I didn't like the sound of any of them. And did I hear him say cats? What cats? I thought I was going to my new furever family to be their one and only special cat. Oh dear – things were going from bad to worse, and I just wanted my mother. I didn't feel brave at all. Or special. Or anything else. I was confused by it all and wondered what I'd gotten myself into. But one thing was clear, I certainly didn't have any say in the matter, and the tiny female human acted like being contagious was the most normal and wonderful thing in the world. She petted me in loving reassurance, picked me up, and gently put me back into the jail. Then off we went into the moving thing again.

After what seemed like a half-mile eternity, we finally stopped and the tiny female human removed my jail from the backseat of the moving thing, awkwardly struggling to hold me while shutting the heavy door. She walked a few steps as gently as she could, still holding my prison as I slid from side to side from her clumsy juggling, and then I heard a door open and quickly close. She walked a few more steps – then another door opened and just as quickly, closed.

I felt my jail lower itself until it hit solid ground, and the next thing I knew, the doors to my prison were opened and the tiny female human was coaxing me to come out. I hesitated, not quite believing her intentions after our previous stop, but curiosity and her trusting eyes got the best of me and I ventured out.

Oh my goodness! Surely I was dreaming! It was the most beautiful place I could've ever imagined, and my eyes went wide with amazement as I took it all in. It was a big room, much bigger than any room I'd ever seen, with sunshine splashing in through the windows – something I rarely saw in the room I had shared with my mother and my siblings. And the floor! It was covered in a thick, plush material that felt like hundreds of dreamy pillows on my little paws. Cat toys were scattered about as well as a brand new litter box just the right size for me! And if that were not enough, also sitting on the floor, tucked away in a cozy corner, was a tiny white wicker basket with a soft cushion inside, perfect for me to nap in and to make biscuits with my little kitty paws!

"Here you go sweet boy," the tiny female human said. "This is your new home for now, and I hope you like it. You're my special little kitty, and I promise I'll take good care of you. I love you, and one day soon you'll meet the rest of the family."

My very own basket, just the right size for me!

Special. She called me special. Just like my mother said I was. I quickly forgot about the prison and the male human with the white coat and the fact I was sick and in quarantine. All I cared about was her telling me I was special. I'd worry about meeting the rest of the family later, so I started to relax. My legs were still a little wobbly from the whole moving thing, but I gained my bearings and started to walk around to check out my new surroundings. Everything my mother had said was true, and at that moment I desperately wished she could have been here with me to share in this wondrous experience.

Meeting the Family

I WISH I COULD TELL YOU I remember my new beginnings with a lot of detail, but it was such a long time ago. A lifetime, really. I remember my special room and thinking I couldn't possibly be a luckier kitten. A kitten with my own bed and my own litter box, lots of fun toys, and a human servant who brought me yummy food and fresh water every day. I remember all that. And I remember some moments of torture, like when the female human picked me up and squirted horrible liquids into me – one liquid was squirted into my left eye, causing me to blink furiously, and the other was served unceremoniously down my throat, causing me to protest with choking noises. With my squirming body, I'm not sure how successful her efforts were, but she was so gentle about it, constantly apologizing as she was torturing me, telling me it was for my own good, so I couldn't stay mad at her for too long.

And even though I couldn't tell you when it happened, one day it stopped. I wasn't sneezing or coughing anymore, and my eye started to clear up. The tiny female had stopped with the torture, and lo and behold, the door was opened. Instead of quickly closing it as usual, she kept it open a crack.

I don't think I ran out of the room immediately, after all, I did have my own comfortable and secure world and had no reason to want more, but I felt a rush of senses – sights, smells, sounds – and it hit me all at once. I was not alone. And then I remembered the big guy with the white coat who had poked me all over the place – the vet. I vaguely recalled him saying something about cats in the plural sense, and darn it if he wasn't right. I saw several sets of diamond slanted eyes peering at me from the distance – no mistaking they were cats like me, but I sensed something else. Dogs! I would remember that unpleasant and vile smell anywhere! Cats I could understand, but nobody had told me there would be dogs here, too!

Okay. Even though I was still a kitten, I tried to remain calm and did my best to look like a tough and no nonsense cat not remotely interested in, or scared of, the several sets of eyes sizing me up from a distance. I kept telling myself over and over that I was special and that I could get through it.

It was easier said than done, but I needn't worry – the female human was clearly used to this sort of thing and already had everything under control. There appeared to be a method to her madness. From what I could tell, there were four of these feline creatures, and she let them come up and sniff me, one at a time, but only for a few minutes so there would be minimal hissing and fur flying over territorial issues. She called this the "acclimation process," but when it comes to kittens, we tend to be a bit more adventurous and curious. So despite what I hoped was my aloof and tough exterior, I actually spent my time trying to make friends by getting to know everyone. Growling and hissing had never been my thing, and I hoped no one would notice my lack of aggressiveness.

The first cat I met looked like she had plans for the night, so I didn't want to take up too much of her time. She was elegantly dressed for a formal dinner, wearing a white tuxedo bib and white gloves against the jet black of her fur. Her name was Shami. I immediately started to babble about how pretty she looked and asked her where she was going. She just laughed and told me she wasn't going anywhere – she always looked like she was going to a fancy supper. She explained that she was named Shami as a variation of Shumu, the famous orca from Sea World, because that is what her markings looked like to the female human. Since I had no idea what an orca was or why it was living at a Sea World, I had no choice but to believe her. Anyhow, it didn't really matter. She seemed nice enough, and I liked her right away.

There was another black and white cat and she was pretty, too, but her fur was not as formal as Shami's and was a bit disheveled. She didn't have a tuxedo or gloves, but she did have the amazing distinction of having the letter "W" brandished on her side, hence her name, Whitney. Even though she was fully grown and older than me, Whitney was a tiny cat and was really shy. I tried talking to her, but once I found out her name, she scurried off to mind her own business. She wasn't necessarily friendly, but she wasn't mean either, so I considered that a victory. So far so good.

The next cat that came by was all black, and I almost didn't see her, but her brilliant emerald eyes gave her away as she studied me to determine if I was friend or foe. Her name was Tosha, and like Whitney, she was a cat of few words so after giving me a cursory sniff, off she went without giving me a second thought.

The last cat I met didn't have any unusual or distinctive markings – she was some sort of brown tabby – and I could feel a wisdom and unassuming confidence radiate from her. While she was not a massive cat, she was bigger than the others and seemed to be in charge. She wasn't bothered by me at all – not one hiss and barely a second glance. I got the sense she had been through this before and was not surprised to see me. Calmed by her demeanor, I began to relax and found myself asking her, without even thinking if it was polite or not, without even knowing her name yet, what the story was with what appeared to be two dogs looking at me.

"Um, excuse me," I whispered as loudly as I could in a tumble of words. "Are those dogs? Are they going to chase after me? And what's your name?"

She inched closer to me, sizing me up with her round, grayish-green eyes. "Whoa, kid," she laughed. "Slow down! One question at a time. Kit's the name and it's nice to meet you. Been wondering when they were going to let you out of that room – sure did take them long enough."

She continued, "Anyhow, kid, don't you worry about those dogs. We cats took care of training them ages ago, and they know who's in charge here. Sure, they'll bark at you and try to chase you around, showing off like a bunch of wild hyenas, but one quick whap on the nose with your claws and those dogs will learn not to mess with you. And even though it's not a cat's place to admit it and you didn't hear it from me, they actually aren't so bad; you might even decide you like them."

Sharing a meal with Kit, Shami, Whitney, and Tosha

The first one I saw was so beautiful she took my breath away, and I couldn't imagine ever whapping her on the nose or anywhere else. She was nothing like the tiny, smelly, yapping brat I knew from living with my mother. According to Kit, she was a Golden Retriever and her name was Bailey. Her silky fur was a warm honey color, and she had a gorgeous mane of a tail that looked like feathers spun of pure gold. It was clear that not only did Kit adore her, but so did the female human, and Bailey was so sweet and good natured that I couldn't help but feel the same way. She was only a puppy herself, a baby like me, and she playfully wagged her wispy tail in a greeting. Our friendship was sealed then and there, and in that moment I realized Kit was right and the dog thing wasn't so bad after all.

The other dog was much more of a character – he was smaller than Bailey and was called Bandit because of the dark mask around his eyes that made him look like an old time bank robber. He puffed his chest out to show his dominance but looked so silly doing it I had to hold my paw over my mouth to keep from meowing out a giggle! He was also head over heels in love with Bailey and fancied himself a big, tough dog that she found irresistible.

Joe holds me as I introduce myself to Bandit and Bailey

Bless Bailey – I swear to the catnip gods she actually winked at me, letting me know in one quick glance what he really was – a small mixed breed of a dog that she towered over and could've easily beaten in a game of pull-the-sock if she so chose, but she was such a polite and refined girl that she always let Bandit win because she loved him and didn't want to wound his silly pride.

So yeah, Bandit sniffed me, barked at me, and chased me around like Kit said he would. Sigh. Dogs can be *so predictable*. But it was harmless and I realized I had nothing to fear. Being the dignified kitten I was, I also took the high road like Bailey and scampered off to hide under the couch to let Bandit think he had scared me, which was the furthest thing from truth. Some dogs sure were easy to manipulate!

Kit's Story

ONCE I HAD FREE REIN of the house it didn't take long for me to settle into my new life with my new family. I had decided to call the tiny female human "Mom" after some convincing from Kit that using that term didn't take away from the love I felt for my furry birth mother. The family also included another human who was male and was Mom's husband and two other male humans that were smaller than Mom – they were her children and she called them Chris and Joey. And of course, there was Kit, Shami, Whitney, Tosha, Bailey, and Bandit.

Life was a constant blur of everyday commotion for the humans – school, homework, birthdays, holidays, out-of-state family visits, jobs, errands, housework, and everything in-between. Those of us with fur were in the thick of it all, constantly underfoot as Mom would say, and every day was filled with the normal chaos of getting through the day.

Nothing stands out in particular, and I don't have one knock-your-socks-off-wow memory, although I do recall I was quite the wiz with a wadded-up ball of paper. I don't remember how it all started – maybe it was from watching

Bailey carry tennis balls all over the house – but once I realized that if I brought a wadded ball of paper in my mouth back to the person who threw it, they would throw it again, it became my all-time favorite game. Eventually my love of fetch evolved to playing tennis, and Mom and the boys would throw the ball of paper up in the air for me, which provided them endless minutes of entertainment as I jumped up and batted it back to them like a seasoned tennis pro!

Other than that, I don't remember anything out of the ordinary – all I know is that whatever was going on, I was a part of it. Mom took all kinds of pictures to document these comings and goings, and more times than not, I was in one of them. Sometimes it was just me, or it would be me with one of the other cats, or me with one of the dogs, or me with Mom, or me with one of the boys. Sure, sometimes there might be a hiss or raised hair here and there, but for the most part, I was extremely content with my life – I had everything I could ever need or want and had no yearnings or desires for anything else.

I especially loved Kit and all the grand stories she told me. It seems she had led a very adventurous life and had come from a place in another land, far, far away from the house in Florida where I was born, from a mystical place she called Upstate New York. Kit said she was a cat of the streets and didn't know or remember who her mother was. Nobody ever told her she was special when she was a kitten and she had to take care of herself all on her own. If she was hungry, she had to hunt for her food and if she was tired or cold, she had to find a warm and dry place to sleep for the night. She couldn't remember anything but trying to survive, and until she met Mom, she didn't have a human to pet her, play with her, or comfort her.

When Kit first told me this story, my eyes grew wide as I couldn't imagine anything so scary and thought Kit had to be the bravest cat in the whole world to go through what she did. Not remember your mother or be told you're special? Not have a warm basket to sleep in? Hunt for food? It was impossible for me to comprehend, yet sometimes if I saw a lizard get into the house, I had an inexplicable urge to chase, kill, and eat it, and I didn't know why. Kit said because we lived with Mom, we had no need to hunt for our food, but the instinct for a cat to want to hunt and kill prey for survival never goes away and that my feelings were normal. I just listened to her in awe, completely enraptured by her worldly experiences and years-beyond-her-age wisdom, and I could only dream of being so wise myself one day.

Since my mother had already advised me I would be a wise cat one day, I knew it was important for me to pay attention to what Kit was saying, not to mention I really enjoyed her stories, so I always begged her to continue with her tales. I was especially interested in how she had finally come to meet Mom, the one thing we had in common.

Always happy to share her stories to an appreciative audience, she jumped up to her favorite spot – the windowsill in the dining room that overlooked the backyard – and gave her front paws a quick washing before she settled in to continue her tale with me. For this one, regarding Mom, she told me it was very cold where she lived. So cold she couldn't even explain it to me because I was a cat who only knew the balmy and tropical temperatures of Florida, and the coldest thing I had ever experienced was when the air conditioner turned on to make the warm air more comfortable in the house or when someone opened the refrigerator door, expelling a temporary blast of frigid air!

She continued on saying that not only was it cold, it also rained all the time and the days were starting to get dark more quickly as it was nearly winter time. It was becoming more difficult for her to find food, and she was growing hungrier by the day. She decided to try out a neighborhood she had never been to before to find a meal and wandered up a driveway, hoping to catch a lucky break by finding a scrap of leftover food in a garbage can – maybe a piece or two of chicken still stuck on the bone – rather than having to exert the energy looking for a poor mouse to kill.

Kit said she was so busy foraging around for something to eat she didn't know she was being watched, but she was – by our Mom. Yup, apparently Mom was no stranger to hungry stray cats because not only did she not shoo Kit away, she went inside and a few minutes later came back out with a bowl of kibble.

Kit paused for a moment before she went on, almost like she was reliving the moment and continued on to say she did her best to pretend she didn't like Mom and didn't want the handout, but her rumbling and empty stomach said otherwise, and the next thing she knew, she'd gobbled up the food in a split second. And horror of horrors, she found herself coming to Mom afterward to be petted! Kit said Mom was just so kind she couldn't help but trust her and succumbed to the gentle caresses of Mom's hand on her fur for a brief, blissful moment.

Oh! This was just too delicious for words, and I had to hear more! Kit stretched, changing the position of her body to adjust to the remaining sunbeam of the day and proceeded to tell me about it like it had happened yesterday. She said that just as quickly as she let Mom pet her, she ran off into the dark of the night. But not only was our Mom smart, she was tricky, too. She knew Kit didn't have a home, so she started leaving food out in the driveway for her. It was supposed to be a secret because Mom already had a house full of other cats like Kit – other cats that seemed to come out of nowhere to find Mom, which would subsequently result in them having a furever home with her. But this time was different because Mom had already been warned by the human husband: *"No more."*

Oh geez – I was on pins and needles by now – her story had me anxious to get to the end, but I sat quietly as she continued. Kit told me it was after the third bowl of food Mom left out that she realized she was tired of being cold and hungry and needed to take matters into her own paws. She kept remembering how it felt to have food in her belly and to have Mom pet her and talk to her with a soothing and gentle tone. And so just like that, she boldly ventured up the driveway and kept on walking until she found herself on the front porch where Mom lived. She knew nothing of the "no more" warning and peered inside the front window where she saw Mom watching TV with the human husband.

My eyes widened in anxious anticipation as Kit continued with her story. It was starting to rain heavily, she said, and she knew Mom saw her outside the window. Kit said she didn't mean to do it, truly she didn't, but a sad and pitiful meow escaped from her cold and tired body. Mom heard the cry but had already promised the human husband she was not feeding the cat and wouldn't bring it inside even though she knew the kitty was homeless (Mom had already put a "found cat" ad in the paper and had been knocking on doors to see if anyone had lost a cat) because if she did, sure enough they would have another pet cat.

I could barely stand the suspense and was on the edge of my seat waiting for Kit to finish her story. She went on to say that despite Mom trying to stay strong, Mom began to cry because it made her so very sad to see Kit outside, homeless, with nowhere to go.

"Oh no, Kit!" I cried out. "What did Mom do? How will this end?"

"Oh, you young and silly boy," Kit laughed at me. "You still have so much to learn. Our Mom is a very special person, and she just so happens to be a beacon for those broken creatures that need her most. Whether it is a place to sleep, love, a meal, a helping paw, or a new home – she gives them what they need. Somehow we're able to find our way to her, and if we put our faith in her, she'll persevere for us. And sure enough, the human husband sensed her sadness and got up from the couch. He opened the door, picked me up, walked back inside, and placed me on Mom's lap. I've been with her ever since and so will you."

Getting Impatient

THE MORE KIT TOLD ME about her life, the more I came to understand what she meant about Mom being a beacon for animals that needed help. It turns out Shami, Whitney, and Tosha had also found their way into Mom's heart and home in Upstate New York as well as countless other cats and dogs. Kit spoke fondly of those she personally knew, who had long since passed to the Rainbow Bridge, like Bo, a devoted and loyal German Shepherd that came from a shelter, and Friday, a sickly tabby cat rescued from a pet store as a "birthday present" for the human husband.

There was also Scooter, a guinea pig Mom rescued from an eminent death sentence from someone she used to work with who shared a cultural belief that differed from hers (the co-worker envisioned the guinea pig as a dinner entrée to be served with a side of boiled potatoes and Mom emphatically did not). There was even a baby bunny that happened into our yard one day. The human husband found it and made the mistake of showing it to Mom – moments later the household had a pet bunny.

Kit continued on describing those she had never met who had been in Mom's life but were at the Rainbow Bridge, like Meagan, a cat Mom had found as a weeks-old kitten, abandoned in the thick of winter at the bottom of a dry well when visiting family in Connecticut, as well as Scrubby, a sweet little polydactyl cat born with only one eye and limited vision in the other. She was stunted at birth and was the runt of a litter that had come as the result of one of Mom's cats who had become pregnant before she was spayed.

Mom felt an immediate connection and protective bond with Scrubby because she had been a misfit at one time herself, too. She was constantly bullied in school because she was a runt – she was always the shortest kid in class and wore thick, coke-bottle glasses, causing the other kids to call her mean names and pick her last for any gym class activities. Naturally, she had an affinity for the underdog (or undercat in this case) and rooted for Scrubby's survival.

When she took Scrubby to the vet for the first time, Mom was horrified to learn that he thought she was there to put Scrubby to sleep. With an indignant and proud resolve, Mom quickly took her home, and Scrubby lived a joyful, happy life with Mom for over 10 years before she had to be helped to cross the Bridge, never once knowing or caring she had a disability or was different.

Even though I hadn't met most of the other animals in Mom's life, I always enjoyed having Kit tell me about them, and it made me happy to know she kept their memories alive in her heart. But, again with the Rainbow Bridge. I didn't know what it was – I made a mental note to ask Kit to explain it to me one day – right then my curiosity was piqued, as I wanted Kit to tell me *my* story.

"If all these cats, dogs, bunnies, and guinea pigs came to Mom," I said to Kit, "then how did Mom come to find me?"

I was never lost and didn't live on the streets, so what was my story? I didn't want to be rude and tell Kit that I wasn't interested in her stories about herself or the others anymore, but I was becoming impatient, wondering about my own.

Patiently waiting for Kit to tell me about my story!

Sigh. Kit was prattling on, back to her story, telling me how, after many days and nights of living with Mom, the other humans, and an assortment of dogs and cats, one day a big truck showed up in the same driveway where she had found Mom. She said the house had been mysteriously overflowing with boxes in every room, some stacked up high to the ceiling. But Kit said these weren't your typical boxes to nap in and explore. These boxes were off limits – they were packed full of human stuff and taped shut so no cat could get inside them! Little by little, the *entire* house was put into boxes until the house was one big, empty, echo chamber with nothing in it because all the boxes were taken out of the house and put into the big truck.

With that, Kit's meow became stronger, and I temporarily forgot I wanted her to stop talking about herself! She quickly rose from her relaxed position on the windowsill and stretched anxiously to tell me the unthinkable. She said without any warning whatsoever, all the cats in the house were scooped up and stuffed into little prisons, just like the one Mom used on me when she first brought me to my new furever home, and were shoved into the backseat of the family car as unwitting passengers to lands unknown. Bo was also in the car and it was a dreadful ordeal as the human husband drove endless hours, traveling from Upstate New York to Florida, which was going to be their new home.

Kit went on to explain it was all so complicated. Mom and the human boys were already in Florida – they had flown in something called an airplane so they could arrive early and find an apartment for us to live in. The human husband had one of his brothers follow him to drive the big, scary moving truck that had the boxes with our stuff in it.

On and on Kit went, and I could barely keep up. Finally I couldn't take it any longer! "What about me?" I blurted out. "How did I get here? Do you know the answer to that?"

My Story

AS USUAL, I need not have worried. Kit knew *everything* and she didn't seem to mind me hurrying her story along at all – she just laughed at my curiosity and impatience.

"Well, kid," she said with a playful glint in her eyes. "I just so happen to know *exactly* what your story is. The simple truth of the matter is that you very well could have had a different life were it not for a chance moment in time. But, just like me finding the right driveway at the right time, when it comes to Mom, some things are meant to be and that is what happened with you."

Oh no! My life with Mom and the rest of the human family could have never happened? I didn't know if I wanted to hear my story after all. Even though Kit was laughing, it was far too upsetting to think that all the loving, toys, and good food might never have been. Or that I never would have met my four-legged friends, Kit, Bailey, Shami, Whitney, Tosha, and Bandit.

"Oh, just relax," said Kit, sensing my anxiety. "You're here, aren't, you? So obviously your story was meant to be –

stop being such a worry wart and lay your furry body down while I think about where to begin."

I obediently did what she said and soon I felt a weird sensation – almost like I could hear my mother whispering to me. "My darling boy," I heard her say. "I know you're still an impatient kitten who's enjoying life – all the fun and the grand stories – but you must slow down a bit and look around you. You're growing into a fine young adult cat, and one day you'll be the one telling stories and teaching cats younger than you about life. Just listen to what she tells you – she knows as I did that you are a special cat and that your story was meant to be."

I cautiously lifted up my head, not sure if I was imagining things, and silently wondered if Kit heard my mother, too. I felt too timid to ask, so I just lay still, nervously washing my ears with my front paws I had wetted with my rough tongue, and waited patiently for her to begin.

She started by telling me it was all rather ordinary. Mom was busy doing Mom stuff – watching the small human boys, cleaning the house, laundry, and things like that. She never sat down to watch television during the day, but she did like to have it on in the background. During this particular day, she happened to have on a channel that was new to her – it was called Animal Planet and had a show on that featured a different cat breed each episode. The breed they were talking about was called a Ragdoll, which was a cat Mom had never heard of, so it caught her attention and she sat down for a minute to see what this new cat was all about.

Once she sat down, she didn't move for a whole hour because she was completely mesmerized by what she saw and heard! Mom knew a lot about cats, but she had never seen a more beautiful breed in her life. It was a stunning cat that wore a silky fur coat in scrumptious, muted tones of coffees, caramels, chocolates, mochas, and creams. To her, the Ragdoll looked like a blue-eyed mixture of a Persian, Siamese, and Burmese all rolled into one incredible cat, and she was fascinated to hear they were known for their docile temperament and tendency to go limp and relaxed when picked up. Mom was so smitten with every aspect of this particular breed she knew she must conceive of a plan to have a cat like this in her house as quickly as possible!

Kit had to say "conceive of a plan" because even in Mom's world where cats just had a way of wandering into her life, she knew the likelihood of a cat she'd never heard of before she saw the show on Animal Planet finding her anytime soon was slim to none. So, without further ado, she announced to the other humans in the household that she knew what she wanted for Mother's Day, which conveniently was right around the corner, and she proceeded to put "Get Mom a Ragdoll for Mother's Day" into motion.

Well, anyone who knows Mom knows she can be both the most patient and impatient person in the whole world. When it came to cats, impatience was the yardstick, and she immediately began scouring the local newspaper classifieds to look for Ragdoll kittens. Yes, it's true! Mom used to live in a time without computers and the Internet and that was how people found things back then! And it was not a quick process either. The breed was relatively new to the mainstream, and it took a couple of months of her looking every day to see if Ragdoll kittens were available. Then one day, it happened! She found an ad for Ragdoll kittens for sale!

Mom couldn't believe her dream of getting a Ragdoll was finally going to come true! She called the people in the newspaper ad and told them she wanted to come see a kitten right away. They gave her directions – it was a long way from the house – almost two hours of driving just to get there, but Mom didn't care. She wanted a Ragdoll and that was that.

"And that's how it all started," said Kit.

This would be me within the year! No wonder
Mom was so smitten with the Ragdoll breed!

Learning About the Rainbow Bridge

I WAS SO EXCITED to know I had my own adventure and my own special story. Granted it didn't have the same pizzazz as Kit's, but it was mine, and I was pleased to know how much Mom wanted me – had she not seen that ad, my life could have been very different and that got me to wondering about my life again. I knew how Shami and Whitney got their names, and I also found out Kit was named by Mom for her love of the Kit Kat candy bar, so how did I get my name?

Kit said that for Mom, naming us pets was quite the ordeal, and she took the task very seriously. The thought process was endless, and the name had to be perfect to suit our personalities, our colorings, or something that just felt right with Mom. I happened to be a Chocolate Bicolor Ragdoll like my mother, meaning my ear tips were dark like rich chocolate and well-defined in coloring, with my body patterned in patches of white and light tans. My face had a dapper mask around my eyes like a raccoon with an inverted white "V" down my nose.

Since my colors ranged from dark brown to white, originally she thought my name would be something inspired by a delicious cup of latte or hot chocolate to match the muted tones of my fur. The only problem – since I was still a kitten when she got me and my fur was mostly white at the time and would take at least a year or two for my full color pattern to develop, the name "Mocha," "Java," or "Cappuccino" just didn't cut it.

Kit said Mom wrote down a list of all kinds of names for me, but eventually my personality was the deciding factor. I was just such a sweet-natured, happy-go-lucky kind of cat that made everyone smile to be around me.

"Jazz," Mom said one day. "That's it. No one can listen to jazz music without feeling upbeat and happy and that's how this little guy makes me feel."

I loved Kit's explanation and I agreed with Mom – it was the perfect name for me!

And that's how it stayed for quite a while – a perfect name for a perfect life that continued in its whirlwind pace of every day running into the next of being a cat who lived with other cats, dogs, critters, and humans. But then things started to change. One day I couldn't find Bailey and asked Kit where she was.

Kit was enjoying a few bites of kibble and looked up from her dish. "Oh," she said. "I thought you knew. Bailey told Mom it was time for her to go to the Rainbow Bridge."

What? What was with the Rainbow Bridge again? And what did Mom have to do with it? I vaguely remembered Kit talking about it before, but I didn't know what she meant and at that time I didn't want her to know I didn't understand her. But now I was older, and I had a nagging feeling my mother had mentioned something about a Rainbow Bridge and teaching the humans lessons about it. But I was such a kitten back then and it was so hard to concentrate on anything except playing with my wadded-up paper balls, snuggling with Mom, and having fun with the other cats. The Rainbow Bridge was not part of my everyday life, so I hadn't thought to ask about it again.

"What's the Rainbow Bridge?" I whispered to Kit. "Can I go and see it with Bailey, and why is she not here at home with us, and why did Mom have to take her?"

"Jazz," said Kit. "Those are very complicated questions and the simple answer is yes, you can go see the Rainbow Bridge and Bailey, just not now. It's not your time yet. And Mom had to take her because it was her way of letting Bailey know how much she loved her."

If I was confused before, I was even more confused now. Rainbows. Bridges. Bailey. Mom. I was having a hard time making the connection and it made me want to meow as loudly as I could.

"Look," said Kit. "I know this is hard for you to understand, so let me try to explain about the Rainbow Bridge as best I can. You and I are here right now. You can see me, touch me, hear me, and we share a good life together with Mom, the other humans, and Shami, Whitney, Tosha, and Bandit. But then sometimes things change. Sometimes one of us pets might get really, really old, or sick, or have an accident like getting hit by a car, and either we are dying, or we are dead. I know you don't understand this – you're young at heart and think you'll be with Mom for ever and ever, but the truth is all of us will die one day, and when we do, there is a wondrous, beautiful place we animals go to called the Rainbow Bridge."

My eyes widened as I tried to take in all of what she was telling me.

Kit gave me a moment to collect myself and then continued with her explanation. "As legend tells it, a lush green meadow is located on the side of Heaven before one enters it. Rainbow Bridge is the name of both the meadow and the adjoining bridge connecting it to Heaven. When a pet or animal dies, it goes to the meadow and is restored to perfect health, free from any injuries. The pet runs and plays all day with the other animals and there is always fresh food, water, and lots and lots of sunshine."

Even though the Rainbow Bridge did sound beautiful, I was still confused and very, very sad. Why was Bailey at the Rainbow Bridge? Mom never let her go anywhere by herself, and she was only about a year older than me, still a baby, really – was I going to die soon and go to the Rainbow Bridge, too? And Bailey was so happy living with us – playing fetch with her favorite tennis ball, swimming in our pool, being Bandit's girlfriend, going to the park, and chomping on doggie bones. I took naps with her all the time, lying next to her soft and silky fur, and we joked about how cute and silly Bandit was. Why would she ask Mom to go live at the Rainbow Bridge when she already had everything she loved and needed right here at our house with all of us? Oh, I didn't like this at all.

Kit continued, trying to help me understand. "Jazz," she said. "Sometimes there are no answers in life that make sense, and you just have to believe there is a greater reason for it all, despite how hard it might be. Even though Bailey was only a scant two years old, she developed something called cancer and was very, very sick. Mom did everything she could for her – she brought her to the man with the white coat for all kinds of tests and medicine and even tried to have the disease removed by amputating Bailey's cancerous leg. Bailey tried to remain strong and cheerful, but no matter what Mom or the man with the white coat did, she wasn't getting better and she was in so much pain."

Kit continued on with a heavy sigh. "Mom kept hanging on, believing that somehow her beloved Bailey would get better because she couldn't imagine a life without her, but Bailey knew in her heart that wasn't going to happen. She knew it would make Mom unbearably sad, but one day she was lying down in the hallway and looked up at Mom. She told her as gently as she could with her eyes that she knew how much Mom loved her but that Mom had to be strong for her. She had to let her go so that she could finally rest in peace and be without the constant pain she was feeling, so she asked Mom to help her cross the Rainbow Bridge."

By now I was crying, listening to Kit as she explained Bailey's story. Kit told me it was okay to be sad and to cry and to even be angry and to think none of it was fair, but she said I also had to understand that what Mom did by helping Bailey cross the Rainbow Bridge was actually a gift from Mom to Bailey that took a lot of strength and courage. Kit went on to say that one day there would be a happy ending for everyone because even though a pet is finally at peace when they reach the Rainbow Bridge, they still miss the guardian they had to leave behind on Earth and wait for them to be reunited.

Bailey already knew from previous talks with Kit what the Rainbow Bridge was all about. She knew the story of how she would be reunited with Mom one day – Kit had explained to her that when a pet guardian dies, they also cross the Rainbow Bridge. At that moment their pet stops whatever they are doing and sniffs the air, looking into the distance where they see their beloved guardian. Excited, they run as fast as they can until they're in the arms of their guardian and they lick their face over and over in pure joy! Their guardian then looks deep into the eyes of the pet that was absent on Earth, but never absent in their heart. Side by side, they cross the Rainbow Bridge together into Heaven, never again to be separated.

Bailey used to love to swim in our pool – I could only hope the Rainbow Bridge had a beautiful one waiting for her...

I could only imagine what Kit was telling me. It sounded like the Rainbow Bridge was far away, and other than my original car trip with Mom to my new house and trips to the place with the guy in the white coat, I'd never been anywhere else. I had no street adventures of survival like Kit did, and despite Kit's explanation, I wouldn't know what a rainbow, or a bridge was for that matter, if they were right in front of me. I tried to imagine beautiful and my mind wandered to Christmas when Mom would decorate the house, and the lights on the Christmas tree would give off a soft, comforting glow – it was so beautiful.

"Is it like that?" I asked Kit.

"Sure," she said. "Beauty comes from the heart, and if that's what beautiful is to you, that's what will be at the Rainbow Bridge and so much more."

I thought to myself that the Rainbow Bridge was both the most beautiful and saddest thing I had ever heard at the same time, but I relaxed a bit from Kit's comforting words and tried to comprehend what she was telling me. I wasn't quite ready to understand the full implications of her lessons, but I did walk away from Kit feeling just the tiniest bit wiser and knew my life was about to embark on a new path.

It All Begins to Change

WE ALL MISSED BAILEY terribly, especially Mom, who took her passing very hard. Bailey was the apple of her eye, and she found it extremely difficult for the longest time to allow herself any feelings of happiness, even though in her heart she knew what she did for Bailey was the right thing. It was just so tragic and so unfair. Bailey was only a baby, and Mom didn't understand why she had to die so young.

Her pain brought me back to the memory of the last conversation I had with my mother – she had mentioned something about us pets only staying with our humans for a brief part of their life, but still being young myself, I considered myself invincible and didn't completely understand the finality of death or why Mom was sad for so long.

In part some of my naïveté had to do with the personality of Bailey herself – when she was alive, she was like a free-spirited sister with me, and I never even knew she was sick because she put up such a brave and cheerful front around me, which Kit said she did because she didn't want to upset or scare me with grown-up talk about a subject as deep and dark as death. She was always a ray of sunshine in our house, and that's how she wanted me to remember her, which is how I did.

And some of it also had to do with Mom – even though the loss of Bailey took a terrible toll on her emotionally, she always had room in her heart to love more animals. Our house became a revolving door of cats and dogs once again as new ones came into our life and old ones passed on. Everyone joked that Mom was like Elly May Clampett of the Beverly Hillbillies, never being able to say no to an animal in need. Some even referred to our house as "a zoo," but Mom always referred to it as a house full of love. All I can say is that it was never lonely for me, and I never really gave Bailey's passing too much deep thought as a result.

Eventually life settled in a new direction – Mom and the human she was married to divorced after 23 years. I didn't really know what that meant, other than that he didn't live in the house anymore. The older human son, Chris, had also moved away to college. Tosha had passed on by now of old age, so at this point I was sharing the household with the younger human son, Joe, as well as Bandit, Kit, and Whitney, along with our newest canine rescue additions – Lexi, a horse-sized red-colored Golden Retriever prone to eating anything in sight; Hobo, a motley-looking grey terrier mix who spent the majority of the day sleeping; and Meadow, a Miniature Pincher smaller than me but with more bark, personality, and spunk than any animal I'd ever met.

Everything was relatively okay for a while until Mom's normally reserved personality started to change, and not even Kit could prepare me for the events to follow the first time *he* came into the house. He was what Mom referred to as her boyfriend, and he was the scariest male human I'd ever met. I could hear him coming from blocks away, the noise of the contraption on two wheels he rode to meet Mom getting louder by the minute until he pulled up to our driveway.

The whole house shook before he arrived, and when Mom opened the door to let him inside the house, I saw him towering over her like a giant. He had a long ponytail trailing down his back like he was a horse instead of a human, and he wore black leather boots and gloves that gave me the shivers. Lexi, Hobo, Meadow, and Bandit all barked in unison in a loud chorus of annoying decibels like a bunch of crazed savages to announce his arrival, as if I were some sort of idiot and didn't hear him coming. Everything about the ordeal was uncivilized, and I wasn't happy with his presence in our household one little bit.

Didn't Mom realize I was a mancat now with a pedigree that deserved respect and some peace and quiet? This was not how things were supposed to be - not to mention, she certainly hadn't asked my opinion on the matter, and all I could do was hope his presence was a figment of my imagination, or at the very least, a one-time-only visit.

Unfortunately, however, I was wrong on both counts. And apparently my aversion was not shared and I was in the minority of opinion because the dogs slobbered all over him like some lovesick slaves, and Mom just floated on a cloud of happiness every time he came by to visit. Rather than participate in the spectacle, I tried my best to remain invisible, but being a big cat at this point, that was not always an easy task. One day he spotted me as I was doing my best to speed past him to safer ground.

"What was that blur of fur?" he asked Mom.

"Oh," she said. "That was Jazz. He's my Ragdoll Cat."

"Wow," said the scary guy who wouldn't leave. "He really is a beautiful cat."

Hmmpf. As if I were buying it for one second. Who did this guy think he was trying to soften me up with compliments? My fur stood on end. I already knew I was beautiful and didn't need a stranger validating that. Deep down I had to admit I was flattered, but I would *never* let *him* know that!

I stood my ground for at least a couple of weeks until one day I found myself doing the unthinkable without being able to control myself. He was standing up, talking to Mom, and I reached up with my big front paws and touched his legs, letting him know I wanted him to pick me up! He immediately reached down, and it happened so quickly I completely forgot I didn't like him. He cradled me like a baby and crooned to me in a soft voice. "Mr. Jazz" he said. "What a good boy you are."

Well, forgive me, but I was as hooked as Mom was, and I could understand why she liked this guy so much. *Mr. Jazz* – I had never been called that before and having such a grand, appropriate, and dignified title bestowed on me had me beaming with pride. I shouldn't have judged him so harshly and quickly, and I was ashamed to admit I should have realized that if Mom felt he was a kind and good person, then I should have given him a chance right from the beginning. I was flooded with the memory of the time when I was a kitten and the female caretaker human told Mom not to pick me because I had a runny eye and a cough. Mom saw past my appearance and loved me for who I was. I was happy I understood the error of my ways, and I think my mother would have been proud of me and my mature conclusion if she were still with me.

From that point on, any time he came to visit, the three of us were inseparable. When he and Mom sat on the couch to watch TV, I snuggled between the two of them, relaxing my fluffy body to the size of a thin envelope, and I stayed there for hours, purring and kneading Mom's soft tummy. It was then and there I decided to call him Dad, without even asking Kit if she thought it was a good idea – it just felt right and it was my own decision. Without even realizing it, I was maturing into a very special cat, and my chest swelled with pride with all the grown-up decisions I was making.

I was glad I was turning into such a wise cat because in the days to come it turned out Mom really needed my friendship. Even though she was happy with Dad and still had Joe living with her, things got tough for her. Within the span of a year, Mom had to find Lexi a new furever home where she could be the only pet because Lexi had become dangerously aggressive around the rest of us. Then Meadow accidently got out of the house and was fatally hit by a car.

Hobo developed cancer and needed help to the Rainbow Bridge, and Whitney passed on to the Rainbow Bridge on her own from old age.

It was just Bandit, Kit, and me now, and the house was pin drop quiet – all of us were past our rambunctious kitten and puppy days, so I was exceedingly grateful when Mom made the decision that it was time to give another animal a good home. Without even thinking twice, she grabbed Joe, her purse, and her car keys, and they headed off to a cat rescue with the intention of picking out a kitten together. What really happened was that the kitten picked them because, according to Mom, out of nowhere a kitten jumped up onto Mom's shoulders, which is how she and Joe knew it was meant to be.

Mom and Harley

She was a pretty little thing and had an orange and black tortoiseshell type of coat with a white bib and mittens. They decided to name her Harley because her colors were like the Harley Davidson motorcycle Dad had. Right off the bat she brought happiness and joy into the house and all was well in our world – that is until once again, life changed.

Maine Coons and Hurricanes

CHANGE WAS HAPPENING, and it was happening quickly. Apparently Dad was no longer just going to be a visitor – he was going to be moving in with us within the next couple of months, which appeared to be a pretty big deal to Mom. She was a bundle of nerves – both excited and apprehensive – and she wanted everything to be just right when it finally happened so Dad would feel like our home was his too and not just a house that belonged to Mom.

Mom had a brainstorm of an idea for the perfect housewarming gift, and rather than go the traditional route like most people – you know, maybe a new bedspread or something like that – she decided he needed a cat of his very own. As it was, even though I loved Dad, I was pretty much a mama's boy. Harley had taken to Joe like glue and barely left his side – she spent most of her time in his bedroom, and if he even so much as got up to use the bathroom she would pine and meow for him to hurry back. And Kit, well, she kind of just liked to hang out on the windowsill in the dining room, presumably reminiscing about her younger days as a badass cat on the streets, so operation "Find Dad a Maine Coon Kitten" went into effect.

Quieter times... Hanging out with Harley in Joe's room

Why a Maine Coon and why a kitten? Well, it seemed when Dad was raising his own human kids, he adopted a Maine Coon rescue cat he named Gonzo and that cat was the cat love of his life. He talked about him all the time, and since Mom knew that was his favorite breed of cat, she felt having a kitten of that breed to grow up with him in his new house would be the most wonderful gift and gesture she could ever bestow on him – kind of like both of them starting a new life together. It sounded like an easy enough plan, but naturally as with any good intention Mom had, it would be easier said than done.

First of all, if we flash-forward in time, even though Mom has loved cats her whole life, it was not until much later in her life that she became who she is today – an author, award-winning blogger, and cat advocate who educates people on the subjects of pet responsibility and spay/neuter. She was not aware of the significant problems of cat overpopulation on the streets and in shelters (the numbers range in the millions if you can imagine that) and didn't think to look for a kitten with a rescue organization. She had assumed if she wanted a Maine Coon, she would need to locate a breeder, so that is what she tried to do.

Unlike with me, where she had to find me through an ad in the newspaper, the Internet was now a part of her world, so she started researching Maine Coon catteries on her computer thinking she would quickly and easily find a kitten with no problem. She wanted him to be just like Gonzo so she looked for a male, and she wanted the kitten to be available before Dad moved in so she could surprise him with a kitten sitting on the bed wearing a big red bow of welcome the day he arrived.

Right off the bat, there were far fewer catteries available within driving distance from Mom than she would have imagined, and she was not about to have a kitten shipped to her from California or something like that. She wanted to meet the kitten in person, and even on a good day she was not a fan of driving in South Florida traffic, so the closer to us, the better. That narrowed the list significantly. Not that kittens weren't available – there were, just not for the timeframe Mom wanted.

After a of couple months of searching, Mom finally found a kitten within a two-hour driving radius that was a male but he wouldn't be available until after the date Dad was scheduled to move in. To make matters worse, Dad was going through a litany of problems of his own and his personal well-being was not in the best shape. Without delving into the details, let's just say life was beating him up and he was not handling it too well, and Mom was scared he might not even move in with us. So despite not wanting to ruin the surprise, Mom felt Dad needed to be told about his gift because if there is one thing she knew, it was that cats have an amazing power to heal the human heart. She knew Dad needed this little being in his life as soon as possible to have something to look forward to.

So she ended up telling Dad about the Maine Coon kitten, and just like she had prayed, he realized he had to put his life back on track and that this kitten and Mom's love would help him do that. Dad would just have to move in without the "surprise" element, and they would pick the kitten up a couple of weeks later, together, when he would be old enough to finally leave his birth mother. It sounded simple enough, but Mother Nature had her own plans, and right before they were scheduled to get the kitten, a category 3 hurricane hit South Florida hard and put everything at a standstill.

This one was named Wilma and oh my gosh did she ever have a temper! I'd been through a few of them before with Mom, but I forgot how scary, loud, and mean they could be. All of us – humans and animals went to bed the night before she was supposed to strike and tried to sleep, but it was nearly impossible. I was on the edge of Mom and Dad's bed the entire night and even though I didn't want to look outside the window, I couldn't help it and saw things I never imagined possible. Gigantic tree limbs, pieces of our fence and endless chunks of debris flew past the window like they were weightless feathers and the whole house shook for hours. It was quite surreal – the noise of the storm outside was incessant, but the inside of the house was eerily quiet because we had lost power at some point.

When Mom and Dad finally woke up after a restless sleep, the house was humid and stuffy because we were still without power and the sky was a foreboding deep grey/greenish color. Dad went outside first before he would let Mom take Bandit out to make sure everything was safe. A tree branch had fallen and broken part of the windshield of Mom's car, another branch had fallen on the roof over Joe's bedroom window, and the whole street was covered in tree limbs and bush debris. I remember my fur feeling sticky because the house was hot and muggy, and it was really hard to get comfortable. Mom kept the litter scooped as best as possible to keep it clean and sanitary for Kit, Harley, and me, but it was a really hard time for everyone. There were no lights, no electricity, and no hot water, and because it was late October, it got dark by 5:00 p.m., and there was no snuggling on the couch because there was no television.

Since the hurricane disrupted our daily routine, I spent most of my time napping in the safety of Mom and Dad's bedroom

So what did this all have to do with Dad and the kitten? Well, lots actually. The plans they had made to pick him up went completely haywire because the place where he was supposed to be picked up from was devastated from the hurricane, and it would be a couple of weeks before the roads would even allow passage to the house he was at. Traffic lights were out everywhere, street signs had been knocked down, and there was a gas and ice shortage. But since Mom and Dad and Joe were so busy cleaning up the yard from all the damage we had gotten from the hurricane and we didn't have power either, we weren't in a rush anymore. Mom and Dad wanted the house to be as safe as possible before we brought a new being into our family, but who knew that the hurricane was the least of it and that a kitten in the house was actually going to be more of a menace than anything else.

Mentoring Zee

WHEN THEY FINALLY brought **HIM** home you would have thought he was Prince William, Duke of Cambridge for all the pomp and circumstance. They went through the usual process that I and endless others had been through – he was shut in a room alone for a while before he was introduced to Kit, Harley, Bandit and me for the standard issue acclimation process. The only difference – unlike the private room I was given when I first came to the house – in his case, he was squirreled away in Mom and Dad's bedroom, and because of that I didn't get to talk to him right away like I wanted to.

I had many questions for him, like did he have a runny eye like I'd had? Did his mother tell him he was special like mine had, and was he expected to teach the humans in his life lessons like I was? Did the house he came from smell and have a dog like the place I came from? All very important questions in my opinion, but we didn't get to meet him for at least a week, only being allowed limited communication as he put his paw under the door to signal to us that he knew we were out there.

Well, actually I should say he was communicating with me to let me know he was behind the door. Although I didn't make the connection right away, if I'd been paying attention, I would have seen that Kit was not by my side, sniffing at our new housemate on the other side of the door. I knew Harley wasn't there – obviously she couldn't pull herself away from Joe's room, and Bandit, well, by now he knew the drill. Mom and Dad would yell at him for sniffing and chasing the kitten because God forbid a dog act like a dog, so he just napped and let the world run its course around him.

When the big day came and I was finally able to meet him, I must admit I was surprised. The way Mom and Dad carried on, I thought he would have been made of catnip and sunbeams, they were so taken with him. Sure, he was cute. Find a kitten that isn't cute, that would be the challenge, I say. But putting it mildly, he was nothing like what I expected. I had once overheard Mom and Dad talking about him before we got him and from what I understood, a Maine Coon cat was supposed to have a regal and luxurious mane like that of a lion in the jungle and a gigantic bushy tail like a raccoon. They were also supposed to be massively big and great communicators!

Since, as I said, Kit, Harley, and Bandit didn't really talk to me all that much anymore, I had to admit I was kind of lonely and was looking forward to having someone to share my day with – someone who actually liked to hold a conversation. I had recently caught a HUGE, DANGEROUS, and SCARY lizard and really wanted to boast about it. Never mind that Dad took the lizard away from me before I could hurt it and that it was actually a tiny, harmless baby lizard. I had learned storytelling from the best, Kit, and I planned on telling this new kitten a whooper of a tale!

Zee when I first met him

Well, color me shocked, but this kitten was scrawny and his fur was short and fuzzy and he didn't meow one word to me! Not even an attempt at a hiss or growl and I was not the least bit impressed. But thinking back to how quickly I had judged Dad, I decided to refrain from comment and did my best to hide my surprise. Too late. He could tell immediately something was off and puffed his little chest out as if to let me know he wasn't a little baby at all.

Oh. It dawned on me at that moment as he tried his best to convince me that he was more than what met the eye, that when I was a young cat, I too was not what I am today. I remembered that my now beautiful fur coat took me several years to develop and that I was the sickly, runny-eyed kitten that "nobody would want" and my heart instantly softened.

"Listen kid," I said, co-opting the title Kit had used with me when she first met me. "I didn't mean to offend you. It's just that I was expecting something different, but it doesn't mean I don't like you. Really – I mean it! One day, sooner than you could ever imagine, you'll be a grand mancat with a thick fur coat like mine and a mane about your face making you look like a wild lion of the jungle!"

He looked at me with his round, owl eyes that were far too big for his tiny kitten face and my heart melted. Bless his soul – he just needed a friend. Poor baby had just been taken from the only life he knew and all of a sudden he was in a new house with new people, new cats, a dog, and new smells. Maybe his mother didn't prepare him for all of this like mine did. Maybe he was just scared and didn't want to admit it.

I decided I liked him, and just like Kit took me under her wings so to speak, I took him under mine. My role in the household was starting to change – without my even realizing it, I had become the top cat in the pecking order. When did this happen, I wondered. As I thought about it, it dawned on me Kit and I had been speaking less frequently than I thought. Oh no! It came to me – Kit was aging and although it had been happening all along, it had been so gradual I hadn't noticed until now, which is why she didn't come out to meet this little guy.

It all started to make sense to me now as I remembered bits and pieces of life with Kit of late – I remembered a phase of time when she seemed really tired and listless and not her usual cheerful self. Yes – it was all coming back to me now – it was before Dad moved in with us, and one night Mom was crying. She had put a blanket on the floor near Kit and lay down next to her all night. She told Joe to tell Kit goodbye, and I didn't know what that meant. Where was Kit going, and why was Mom crying?

But the next day Kit was better. Mom said something about a miracle – whatever had made Kit tired and Mom sad had gone away, so I didn't give it much thought. Kit was back and I didn't think to be alarmed. Kit was always strong and always a part of my life. But that was a couple of years ago, I reflected. Where did time go? All I knew was that with the kitten here, it made me realize life indeed had been changing, as had I. Kit was grooming me to be head of the household, and my protégée was standing at my large and fluffy paws, looking at me with such trust and awe that I immediately flashed back to the first time I met Kit. The feeling was bittersweet.

"Young cat," I said. "Settle in next to me and let's talk – this is a big family and you've got a lot of catching up to do!"

Home Improvement

MOM AND DAD CALLED him "Zee," and I'll admit I didn't quite get the connection at first. Who names a cat Zee? What does that even mean? Isn't that a letter of the alphabet? Surely there must be a rational explanation, and Zee proceeded to tell me that his father was none other than Zeeba – Wizpurrcoon Zeeba of Classic Cats to be more precise – the largest registered male Maine Coon in the United States at 35 pounds! Wow! Thirty-five pounds, I thought to myself. Was he a cat or a small dog?

Anyhow, since the beginning of time, Mom has *always* named all of the animals in our family. But since this particular kitten was a gift for Dad and because Mom wanted Dad to know this was his extra-special gift, she let him pick out the name. Two seconds later without the usual painstaking torture it took Mom to pick names for us, he yelled out, "Zee!" Why? Quite simply, it was the abbreviated version of Zeeba and he felt it was the proper justice to Zee's incredible lineage.

Well, whether Zee would fit into the large pawpads of his infamous father, only time would tell, but in the meantime since it seemed the name Zee was going to stick, Zee it was. To my enormous pleasure, Zee and I began to chat. No, his house didn't smell like rancid urine. No, he had never met a dog, and yes, his mother did love him, but he didn't remember much about her or if she taught him any words of wisdom or lessons. He said her name was Cassandra, and she had told him from the day of his birth that he was born to go live with a human who would want him very much, and he was content with that. He knew he was a cat with pedigreed papers and was proud of his heritage. He didn't have a runny eye or any infections and the only real issue he had was that he hated his fuzzy fur and couldn't wait for his big lion mane to grow so he could look like his great father!

We became very good friends right from the start, and he brought the kitten back out in me. I would tear around the house with him (boy, did he have a lot of energy), and I showed him how I jumped up in the air and batted at wadded-up balls of paper like a tennis athlete (a skill he never picked up). I also showed him how I could stand up on my hind legs to jiggle the handle on closed doors with my front paws to open them, and I really impressed him with my ability to open Mom's dresser drawers and fling her clothes all over the floor for no reason other than that I enjoyed doing it. We would wrestle too, and when we were done we would snuggle on the couch together for a friendly nap.

Life was good, and it settled into a nice routine for our new family, or so I thought. You can only imagine my surprise when a couple of months after Dad had been with us, he decided a complete knock-down-start-from-scratch home renovation that included the kitchen, living room, half bath, den, and dining room was in order. The ordeal was one I will never forget, and for those of you who might not be aware, all I can say is that when a home renovation happens, there is literally no turning back and life becomes completely out of control, topsy-turvy.

I was a cat that preferred routine, cleanliness, quiet, calm, schedules, and order. None of those things exist during a renovation, and our house was in complete rubble and disarray for months as wall after wall went crashing down at the hands of what I thought were my gentle humans. Loud, and jarring noises emanated inside my once peaceful house for hours at a time as old ceramic tiles were jack-hammered up and hardwood planks were yanked out. The carpet that felt so good on my paws was also pulled, and the popcorn ceilings I liked to stare up at were scraped down in a goopy mess. Dangerous electrical wires were moved or replaced, the plumbing was gutted, and on and on through the reciprocal process of studs and drywall being put up to create new walls and rooms, primer being painted on, new ceilings being hung, and so on and so on until a new house had virtually been built from scratch.

We literally lived like nomads during this process as Mom and Dad moved our old furniture and appliances from one spot to another while they gutted room after room, and everything in the house was constantly covered in a thick grit of dust that made my silky fur feel dirty and heavy. Mom and Dad would work on the house until the wee hours of the morning, way past our normal bedtime, and the ordeal was endless. Kit, Harley, Bandit, and I all had to navigate to wherever the furniture was placed at the moment to nap, and

Mom and Dad hardly had any time to pay attention to us anymore. They didn't watch TV at all, so nighttime cuddling was a thing of the past. I desperately missed my old life and just didn't understand what was happening to the house I had loved so much. To me, nothing had been wrong with it, so I just felt bewildered, scared, and confused by all of it.

Harley, Bandit, Kit, and I making do...

Kit, Bandit, and Harley didn't seem anywhere near as bothered as I was – they just kind of went with the chaotic flow and Zee actually loved the whole renovating process. He stayed by Mom and Dad (and by all the strangers who came over to help) every step of the way and was fascinated by every little bit of what was going on. He would stand tall and proud on top of the ladder that temporarily came to live in the house, and sometimes his tail would have paint, spackle, caulk, or primer on it from helping. He truly thought the whole thing was one great big grand adventure on a ship he was captain of. I wish I could have been more like him, but

Zee didn't have the same connection to the house I had and he didn't understand my adverse reaction to any of it.

The worst moment for me was the first night. I remember that out of nowhere, Mom and Dad put Harley, Kit, Zee, Bandit, and me into their bedroom and shut the door like we were being punished. Did we do something wrong that I unaware of? I didn't think so, but by this exasperating point, I wasn't so sure. Normally I could open a closed door with relative ease, but when I tried wiggling the door knob, this time, nothing happened. It seemed they had latched the door with a lock, so whatever was going on was serious business.

Bandit settled down right away on the bed, something he would normally get yelled at for and Harley hid behind the headboard. Kit joined Bandit on the bed, and Zee and I stood guard by the door, wondering what would happen next. And then, a few quick moments later, we heard a loud noise, like a hammer hitting a wall, and it happened over and over for hours. Neither of us had any idea what was going on, and when they finally opened the door to let us out, I was shocked at what I saw and stopped dead in my tracks.

The dining room area – an area that was supposed to connect two rooms with a series of archways and cut out window ledges was completely gone. The archways and walls had vanished into thin air like magic, and all I could see was a pile of dozens of garbage bags filled with the remnants of a world I used to know on the floor. My whole life flashed before me, and I wailed in pain. Where were the ledges that I used to nap on and that Mom used to put her keys on? Where were the walls that separated the rooms and acted as a backdrop to my favorite couch?

I was beside myself and began pacing back and forth, looking up and down to try to figure out what had happened, and I meowed the most primal and mournful sound I could to convey the intensity of my loss. I tried desperately to calm myself, but I could feel my whole world crumbling around me and just didn't know what to do. My life had always been so orderly – occasionally people would come to visit and disrupt my routine – one time Kit accidently got outside and was gone for a whole night which made Mom crazy, and another time Whitney went missing but was actually hiding in the bookshelf behind the TV, but that was really about the extent of it.

A pile of rubble – that is what my house had turned into. Could you blame me for being upset that my world was turned upside down?

This was beyond upsetting, and my mother never prepared me for anything like this happening in my life. After crying for a few minutes, I felt Mom and Dad next to me. They were talking to me, petting me, and reassuring me everything would be okay. They told me they understood I was sad, confused, and upset, but life would make sense again soon and peace and harmony would again be restored to my world.

Once this was all explained to me, I felt my body start to relax, and I decided to trust Mom and Dad. They had never let me down before, so why should this be any different? Nobody else was panicking, not even shy Harley, so I decided rather than get upset, I would be more like Zee and get involved. Now mind you, not involved to the point I was going to subject myself to getting paint or whatever on my tail – getting dirty was not my thing – but I could still participate. So what I ended up doing was spending the renovation part of the day napping safely in the distance, and then I would come out at night when Mom and Dad were done for the day to inspect what they had accomplished.

I had to admit I really liked this setup – Mom and Dad nicknamed me "Inspector General," and I came out without fail every night and went to the exact spot, room, or location they had worked on that day to look the project over from top to bottom, as if to say, "Yes, good work, this came out very well." I was quite good at my job, and Mom and Dad joked that the job wasn't complete until I gave it my "Mr. Jazz Cat Stamp of Approval."

And you know what, once the renovation was done, I have to say the "new" house was pretty amazing. No more ordinary, boxed-in house – the open floor plan gave Zee and me all sorts of extra room to run and play, and we would zoom around at the speed of light like cartoon characters chasing after each other! Sometimes our legs would be going so fast that zing, like a boomerang, we would collide into a wall before we would ricochet back into a full speed run to continue chasing each other!

And the soft carpet I thought I would miss so much wasn't such a big loss after all. The new tiles on the floor were so nice and cool to lie on and felt wonderful against the warmth of my body. And boy did it make chasing my wadded-up balls of paper so much more exciting than playing on the carpeting because the smooth tile allowed the paper to zip across the floor at breakneck speed!

Zee and I on our new couch!

There were also new shelves and bookcases Mom and Dad made – I wasn't much of a jumper myself, but Zee loved them. And we got a comfortable new couch to snuggle on as well as new kitchen counters to lounge on and so much more! All in all, Kit, Harley, Bandit, Zee, and I loved the new house and things started to get back to normal. Zee and I got back to our games of playing and wresting, and everything was fine until one day out of the blue Zee started to become sort of an obnoxious jerk. Once again, life was on a course heading for a change I didn't ask for.

Farewell My Friend

IT TURNS OUT we didn't notice it because we were all so busy with the renovation, but Zee was no longer a tiny kitten and was getting bigger and stronger by the day. His playtime antics were becoming a lot more physical, and he didn't realize how aggressive he was with me. Sometimes I meowed in protest when he rabbit kicked me to the ground, which made Mom and Dad yell at him. I swear I wasn't trying to get him in trouble, but he really was getting out of hand. One day I got so mad at him, swatting at him to leave me alone, that Mom and Dad actually picked him up and brought him into their bedroom and closed the door.

"Zee," they said in unison. "That was really naughty – you're getting a time out, and we're not opening the door until you behave."

Oh geez – this was a dilemma. He was so annoying, but he was also my friend and I didn't like getting him in trouble, so I snuck past Mom and Dad to open the door to let him out. He zoomed out like the speed of light and all was well for the time being – until the next time he got out of hand again. I warned him he better knock it off or he would get in trouble, but it was too late. Back into the bedroom for a timeout, and this time Mom and Dad smartened up – they watched me to make sure I didn't open the door.

Things started to get worse instead of better. He was like a smart-aleck, know-it-all teenager out of control who needed to be permanently grounded for breaking the rules of the house, and I was at my wit's end with him. Not only was he being a jerk with me, but he was causing all kinds of other trouble – one night he knocked over a set of collectable candlesticks that had been safely residing on the mantel for years, causing them to break in half. Another night he was being such a brat that he deliberately knocked a glass bottle of bright pink grenadine to the kitchen floor to get Mom and Dad's attention because he saw them outside and wanted them to come back in – which naturally they did because thanks to Zee, they now had a dangerous mess of sharp and sticky glass to clean up.

Not only did I disapprove of his uncouth behavior, but I was no match for him physically, and the only solution seemed to be a younger playmate for him to share his excess zeal and energy. I had overheard Mom and Dad talking about the possibility of getting a kitten and had initially thought it was a great idea. But now, I wasn't so sure. My gut was telling me that I couldn't encourage that decision because I knew it wouldn't be fair to Kit – much as I didn't want to admit it, when I forced myself to really look at her, it pained me to see she had become a frail and delicate shell of her old self.

The signs were everywhere that Kit was no longer the strong and resilient cat I remembered – Mom had folded up a large, fluffy towel and put it on the kitchen floor for Kit to lie on. She put it close to our food dishes so Kit wouldn't have to walk far to eat, and she had also brought in a special litter box for Kit to use so she wouldn't have to walk down the hallway to the bathroom where our litter box was. It dawned on me as well that Kit and I never had any conversations anymore, and my heart ached at the realization. She had told me a couple of years ago after her miracle recovery that she wasn't ready to leave this earth and that I would know when it was her time to go. She said her last and final job would be to let Mom and Dad know that she was ready to go and it would be okay to let her. Was that time now, I wondered?

If that was the case, then my dear friend deserved some peace and quiet, and bringing a kitten into a household could be overwhelming to the existing cats even on a good day, so I was relieved when I heard Mom tell Dad the time for a kitten just wasn't right. She wanted to make sure Kit was undisturbed as much as possible for the time being, and a kitten was just not in the cards. Zee was more than enough to handle at the moment, and I was just grateful he never once exerted his over exuberance her way.

As it was, it turned out sooner than later my gut feelings were right. Mom was breaking into tears every time she saw Kit and would constantly whisper to Kit, telling her what a good girl she was and that she loved her. The inevitable was upon us and there was no pretending any longer – Kit was dying, Mom was trying to process it, and it was up to me now to be strong and brave for my loyal friend who needed a furry shoulder to lean on.

"Jazz," Kit whispered to me one day. "Please help me tell Mom and Dad that I want them to let me go and they don't have to feel guilty about the decision – I'm just so tired and my time on this physical earth will be over soon. I want them to know that by helping me cross the Rainbow Bridge they'll be giving me the peace and happiness I've been longing for the past couple of months."

She continued, "Humans just don't have the strength to let us go on their own – they always struggle with the decision, and it's up to us cats to be stronger and braver than they are because the truth is, we're not scared. When we know in our hearts it's time to go, we actually look forward to moving on."

I listened to Kit, her voice so weak I had to strain to hear her. I thought back to the days when she had tried to explain to me why Bailey had left us. I still didn't completely understand what Kit meant. How could I? In the scheme of things, I was still relatively young and had many more years of my life in front of me, and I couldn't imagine being ready, let alone wanting to move on. I couldn't imagine leaving Mom and Dad. Or Harley, Zee, and Bandit. But I was not naive any longer like I was with Bailey. Kit was not the Kit of days gone by and if she was ready to go, I respected her enough to know she spoke the truth, so I vowed to carry out her last wish for her. I owed her that much and knew one day when the time was right, I would understand what she was trying to tell me.

"Okay," I told Kit. "I promise I'll help tell Mom and Dad that you're ready for your trip to the Rainbow Bridge and they need to let you go. I'll let them know they do not have to feel guilty for doing it and you're grateful for the wonderful life you had for so many years. I'll tell them you love them very much and you'll be waiting for them at the Rainbow

Bridge with Bailey and all the others when it's their time to go."

I could feel the weight of the world lift from Kit's bony little body as I gave her my reassurance.

"One more thing," she whispered. "Please, in time, let them get the kitten they want. You might not think I heard them talking about it, but I did. A kitten is a symbol of rebirth and life. Let them revel and celebrate the joy it will bring back into the household. But most of all do not ever, ever think it means I was not loved. Humans have a heart capable of endless love, and there is always room for one more animal to love in that heart."

It was at that moment that I realized Kit was saying goodbye to me and this would be our last conversation. My heart swelled with love for her, and I silently vowed to be the esteemed cat she believed I was capable of being.

One of the last times Kit was seen resting on her beloved windowsill

An Improper Love Story

IT WASN'T EASY and it didn't happen overnight, but somehow I channeled the tone of the conversation I had with Kit to Mom and Dad, and eventually Mom had to make the unavoidable call to the place where the human with the white coat was. A short while after the call, Mom gently picked Kit up from the spot on the kitchen floor where she was trying her best to rest comfortably and wrapped her in a towel so she could sit on Mom's lap in the car as Dad drove them to the vet. That was the last I ever saw of Kit.

I don't know what happened next since I didn't go with Mom and Dad, but according to what Kit told me would happen, Mom and Dad would stay with her while the vet helped her cross the Rainbow Bridge. He would do that by injecting a serum into her body that would instantly make her really sleepy, immediately wiping away all of her pain. Mom and Dad would be with her the whole time and would pet her and tell her over and over how much they loved her until that final moment when her heart would stop beating in the physical sense. She said it would be very quick and peaceful and wouldn't hurt her at all. But best of all, she said the last memory she'd ever have would be the comforting words coming from Mom and Dad, telling her how much they loved her. I had no reason not to believe her, and I was glad to know Mom and Dad would be with her to the very end. Kit was such a good friend, and she deserved that respect and dignity.

Even though Kit's crossing had been expected and she had urged us all to move on and not to mourn her passing, the house was deafening in silence for months after she was gone. She had been 18 years old when she died and was such a big part of everyone's life. I tried my best to keep everyone happy, but Mom was a shell of herself and the house became a dark hole, devoid of any life or sprit. Leave it to Zee to break the mood, as one night he had enough of the moping around and snapped all of us back to reality.

If memory serves, it went something like this – Mom and Dad were sitting on the couch, very innocently watching TV, just like any other night. I was tucked in between them, and out of nowhere Zee came running and lunging up from behind us. He used Dad's head as a springboard and propelled himself across the room. Rather than politely retract his claws beforehand, he embedded them deeply into Dad's head and used them as a clamp prior to his launch.

I can't even repeat what happened next. Dad screamed a string of bad words because Zee had sunk his claws so deeply into his scalp that he was bleeding profusely! Poor Dad! But honestly, even though Zee can be a brat, he didn't mean to hurt Dad. He was just so darn bored with us all and was playing. The worst thing you can do to a pet is scold them for doing something instinctive, and it was then and there Kit's wise words came back to me – it was time for that kitten Mom and Dad had been putting off getting and just like that, "Operation We Need a Kitten Now" was put into place, and you don't have to be a mind-reader by this point to know what happened next.

Yup – you know how it is with Mom – once she has her mind set on something, you can bet your bottom dollar it's going to happen – and soon. What Mom had her heart set on was a Bengal kitten. For years she had been mesmerized by the breed and had wanted to adopt one. For those of you who might not know, a Bengal cat is a gorgeous, intelligent, and extremely athletic creature that descends from the Asian Leopard Cat and almost looks like you've taken a full-grown wild leopard and shrunk it to domestic cat size!

I knew all of this because I used to sit with Mom while she looked at pictures of the Bengal on her computer trying to find one to adopt. She would say to me, "Jazz, isn't that a beautiful cat?!" I didn't have much experience with cat breeds, being limited to the cats I'd seen in my own life, but I had to admit she was right – the Bengal *was* a beautiful cat. But they also scared me. What if this cat really was like a wild leopard? Even though Zee didn't look anything like a leopard, he was wild enough, and I wasn't sure Mom was making the right decision.

But Mom was convinced this was the right breed and it was the right time. Zee needed a playmate that could withstand the rigors of his strong personality and that was that. A couple of months later, the sleek ball of fluff Mom and Dad bestowed with the name Zoey entered our lives. She was the most gorgeous creature I'd ever seen, and she was also the tiniest. I immediately wondered what in heaven's name Mom and Dad were thinking. How could this little being possibly be considered a proper playmate for Zee who was a big ole brute of a bully cat? He would eat her alive, and I shuddered at the thought of the ensuing carnage.

Well, darn it all if Mom wasn't right. The moment Zoey entered our home, all rules, boundaries, and normalcy went out the window. Zee took one look at her and was instantly smitten. That obnoxious, overbearing cat became a pliable, bowl full of jelly and instantly lost charge of all his sensibilities. In a nutshell, he was head over heels in love, and Zoey was his one and only.

What did all of this mean for me? Well, I was definitely not picked on anymore. My buddy Bandit, the last-standing dog in our canine legacy, had sadly since passed on to be with Kit at the Bridge and Harley pretty much kept to herself, so as a result, I was kind of on my own and hung out a lot more with Mom and Dad. I still cared for Zee, but he hardly had the time of day for me anymore. He and Zoey were inseparable, and that was fine by me. I was happy to see him so happy, and to be honest, it wasn't that I didn't like Zoey, but she wasn't really my cup of tea and I didn't want to hang out with her.

I was used to female cats being much more lady-like, genteel, and calm. Joe had since moved out, and as a result Harley had finally ventured out into the living room and had taken to napping all day and night on the couch – she was so quiet that sometimes you didn't even know she was around. And Kit, well, she was always so dignified and reserved when she was still with us. Zoey, on the other hand, was a perpetual steamroller of activity – a huntress, acrobat, and athlete – and truth be told, she put all us male cats to shame with her prowess and jumping skills.

A rare moment sharing time with Zee and Zoey together

Not that any of it mattered because the whirlwind romance was short lived to say the least. That's right. Mom, who has since made a name for herself in the world of animal advocacy as one of the top proponents of spay/neuter, who has won awards, and even wrote for *Cat Fancy* magazine, was a naive cat parent at one time and thought a female cat had to be at least a year old before she could be spayed.

Well, wrong, wrong, and wrong. Not only can a kitten be spayed or neutered as young as 8 weeks, but a female cat can conceive as early as 4 and a half months of age. So at 10 months old, after an irresponsible night of unbridled lust, a couple of weeks later it was determined that the young and carefree Zoey was going to be a mother.

Kitten Invasion

IF YOU ASK ME, the whole thing was a complete disgrace, but I wasn't the best one to judge. I mean, sure, I had loved Kit, Whitney, and Shami – all girl cats – but Kit was more like a wise grandmother to me and Whitney and Shami were like sisters when they were alive. And I loved my dear friend Harley, whom I shared my days and nights with, but certainly not in the romantic sense. Not to mention, I was neutered years ago, so I really couldn't relate to what Zee had been feeling for Zoey, and I felt it best not to lecture him. I knew Mom would take responsibility for what had happened, but I had no idea our house, which had finally been restored to a semblance of calm after the renovation and Zee's rambunctious behavior, would be turned so upside down as a result of the pregnancy. But that was nothing compared to the upside down that came as a result of kittens.

Kittens. That's right. Without any warning, after a couple of months of Zoey getting fatter and fatter, early one morning she woke up and felt really funny. Her tummy was giving her some pain and she went into the bedroom to wake Mom to tell her she was ready to have her kittens. And just like that, the bedroom that was always free rein to us cats was strictly off limits to everyone but Zoey. The door was shut with a resounding resolve, and our house became inhabited with the addition of four tiny, high-maintenance beings that bore a striking resemblance to Zoey.

Or at least that's what I gathered from what Zee eventually told me. Neither he nor I actually saw the kittens right away, and that's how we wanted it. Even when Mom and Dad finally opened the door a couple of weeks after they were born to let us peek inside and say hello, it was a disaster. I didn't even bother to go in when given the chance, and when Zee finally dared to investigate, he took one look at Zoey and the kittens, hissed, and left in a discombobulated huff! To her credit, Zoey didn't hiss back – at least not at that particular moment – she just calmly went back to tending to her kittens.

So right then and there the epic Romeo and Juliet love story extraordinaire came to a screeching halt as Zee sized up the situation. He knew something was going on behind closed doors, but he never imagined this – Zoey, *his* Zoey with her sleek body and intoxicating ways was now a mother who was nursing four squirmy little kittens. He was seething with jealousy and mortified by what he had witnessed. When I saw him scurry past me, I felt so bad for him I asked him what had gotten him so irate.

He confided to me that he didn't understand what was going on anymore. Zoey, *his* Zoey, his best friend and playmate didn't care about him anymore. She'd abandoned him and all she cared about was what appeared to be four little beings that looked nothing like him! He felt like they no longer had anything in common, and he resented her newfound happiness. I patiently listened to his rant and didn't feel it was appropriate at the time to point out the obvious to him – they had four kittens in common, he was the father, and they were also his responsibility – so I let him continue his vent with me.

A very dejected Zee...

Poor fellow, he was so forlorn and dejected that even though I wanted to be mad at him and lecture him for being such an irresponsible and reckless cat by falling in love so quickly with Zoey before getting to know her better, let alone getting her pregnant, I just couldn't. Even though Zee had his jerky moments with me, he was still my buddy and I cared about him so I did the best I could to keep up his spirits. Plus I knew a surprise trip to the vet was in order for him to be neutered, and I didn't want to scare him with that news. I also remembered how kind Kit used to be with me when I was scared, confused, or down, and I wanted to return the favor with Zee. I told him things would be back to normal in no time and that Zoey would get tired of the kittens and start paying attention to him again. I honestly didn't know if that was true, but it really didn't matter because I don't think Zee believed a word of what I was saying anyhow.

I tried to remain upbeat, but to Zee's credit, I could understand why he was feeling so lonely and neglected because I kind of was too, although I didn't want to make a big deal out of it like he did. I had faith things would work themselves out, but the truth was, not only was Zoey consumed with her kittens, so were Mom and Dad. They spent every free minute they had with them and Zee and I could hear Mom and Dad laughing and talking behind the closed bedroom door all the time.

Mom, my supposed couch buddy, was especially consumed. Apparently she was helping Zoey take care of the kittens, which required every ounce of her time and energy. As each week went by, she needed to help with new things, such as socializing them (as if it were possible to make them more social – all they ever did was meow and play all day and night), helping them become accustomed to using a litter box, learning how to eat solid food while Zoey was weaning them, and on and on. It was a 24/7 job and the only reason I knew any of this was because during those limited times when Mom and Dad finally did sit and relax on the couch with me, all they ever did was talk about the kittens.

Not that I blame Mom. Zee might, but I did see that she tried to spend time with Harley, Zee, and me and she always made sure we had lots of food, fresh water, and clean litter. It's just that it wasn't like it used to be, and sometimes it made me miss the quieter days when it was just mostly Kit,

Harley, and me. But then I would feel selfish – I knew Mom loved us and it would really hurt her feelings if she thought we weren't happy.

So I tried my best to be upbeat and cheerful. I was a sensible cat, and the kittens seemed to make Mom and Dad really happy – they loved taking pictures of them and it was nice to hear them laughing and giggling all the time. And to be fair, it's not like Zee, Harley, or I had even given the kittens a chance. The kittens were behind closed door for weeks and I honestly didn't even know what they look liked, let alone if they had names or how many were boys and how many were girls.

I decided the best thing to do was to venture closer to the bedroom door and see for myself before I passed judgment. Mom and Dad had started to leave the door open a crack so we cats could watch the new family from afar and get accustomed to having them around. When I finally steeled up the nerve to look closely, I have to admit I was fascinated. Four perfectly formed little creatures were running around the closet floor on wobbly legs. They ran, wrestled, jumped, and climbed nonstop and were so busy they didn't even notice me! It made my head dizzy to watch them, and I politely walked away. Simply put, they were amazing and I could see why Zee was so worried. In the brief moment I witnessed, I saw a very strong and proud mama in Zoey. She was beaming with pride, and clearly these kittens were her love, joy, and priority.

*Zoey was absolutely glowing around her kittens,
but I felt it best not to let Zee know that...*

Rather than tell Zee all of that, I just reported to him that they looked like a bunch of squirmy, noisy brats that Zoey would tire of. I continued by telling him that surely Mom and Dad had plans to find them furever homes with other human families when they were old enough to leave Zoey. After all, he and I had to leave our cat mamas for human homes, so that had to be the case here too. This seemed to make him very happy, and I was relieved he bought my story. Inwardly, I sighed and couldn't shake the feeling that this time I was very, very wrong with my predictions, but I just chalked it up to my being overly anxious, as usual, put it out of my mind, and jumped on the couch for a much needed nap to settle my nerves.

Helping Mom

MY MOTHER HAD TOLD me as a kitten that I was a very special cat and it turns out she was right. I tended to be more perceptive than my other feline housemates, and I should have trusted my instincts because a couple weeks after giving Zee his pep talk, the kittens were released from the bedroom for the first time and were allowed to walk (or should I say, curiously run) down the hallway into the living room that currently belonged to Zee, Harley, and me.

I wish I could lie and say it went smoothly, but it was a horrific ordeal that I will never forget. Fur stood on end on each and every cat and kitten, and a disconcerting symphony of hissing and growling ensued from all of us. Even I mustered up a dignified huff, and Harley woke from her nap on the couch long enough to hiss as well. Now granted, a hissing kitten is not very intimidating, but an overprotective Mama cat growling and lunging at us was.

Mom and Dad were overprotective too, and just as quickly as the kittens were in the living room, they were just as quickly scooped up and brought back to the safety of the bedroom. Everyone was on edge – Zoey was still lashing out at all of us, especially at Zee who was hiding in a corner to escape from her unyielding wrath. She may have been tiny, but Zoey was a force to be reckoned with and her message was relayed loud and clear – STAY AWAY FROM MY KITTENS. Sigh. As if we wanted anything to do with them at that point – not to mention, we weren't the ones who brought them out in the first place. Thanks a lot, Mom and Dad.

But none of it mattered because it became abundantly clear to me at that very moment that Mom and Dad had lost their minds and that these little hellions wouldn't be going to new furever homes. I was certain they would be back in the living room at one point or another because Mom and Dad had that possessive look in their eyes, the one that unequivocally said "we've fallen head over heels in love with these little darlings and couldn't possibly dream of giving them away."

There was no doubt Zee and Zoey's kittens were melt-your-heart adorable!

The truth of it sunk in rather quickly with all of us, even with Zee who wasn't always the brightest bulb in the room. Thinking back to the days when Zee wrestled with me and I got annoyed, I realized how much I missed those days. It was so much simpler then. Zee wrestled. I meowed. He got a time out and got sent to the bedroom whereby I let him out. The house was in absolute turmoil now, and I wondered how Kit would have handled it all were she still with us.

Kit. That cat who had at one point lived with four dogs, a rabbit, and three other cats all at the same crazy, chaotic time. I surmised she would handle it with her typical no-nonsense grace and style. This too will pass she would say and she would always be right. And sure enough, at some seemingly endless point later it did. Mom and Dad, surprise, surprise, kept three of the four kittens – the two girls and one of the boys. The other male was given to a friend of ours who had flown in from Boston for the sole purpose of adopting him. He named him Zeuss Catt and this kitten got the adventure of his life because he got to take a plane ride back to his new home up north! Even Kit with all her grand stories had never flown on an airplane!

The two girls that stayed with us were given the names Mia and Peanut by Mom, and she named the other male Rolz. They were actually quite nice when all was said and done, and it was easy enough to ignore them if I felt so inclined. And truthfully, they pretty much hung out together like stuck glue, so it wasn't like they really were that much trouble or like they bothered me all that much.

Zoey eventually calmed down and resumed her relationship with Zee, albeit not with the same passion, but in a more subdued, comfortable slipper kind of way. And Zee, bless him, even acknowledged the kittens were his and ended up being a wonderful father that the kittens loved, respected, and adored. Mom and Dad ended up on the couch at night like the good old days, and I found myself snuggling on Mom's chest every night like I used to. I wish I could say that all was good, but it was not.

Not that it was bad per se – all of us cats were still well taken care of and loved, but something was off with Mom and Dad. They were always home and seemed really upset and stressed out all the time. They tried to pretend they were okay, but I could sense something was wrong, so I rallied everyone together to see how we could make Mom and Dad happy again.

From what I gathered from the bits of conversation I overheard, Mom and Dad no longer had a job – they were both laid off from the same company on the same day and were scared about losing our house and paying the bills. Since we cats were taken care of and fed every day, we might not have even known anything was wrong, but we can be very intuitive, and I could feel the stress emanating from Mom and Dad. I also knew the value of a cat's love, warmth, companionship, and wisdom to a human, so as the eldest cat, it was up to me to teach the others, especially the kittens who were still too young to understand the ways of the human mind, the importance of giving Mom and Dad extra lap snuggling and purrs.

Mia, Peanut, and Rolz took the day shift, and I must admit they got off to a slow start, what with being overzealous, playful kittens and all. This became evident when Mom decided to take out an old crocheting project of hers to work on to help distract her worried mind. She liked to crochet while watching *The Ellen DeGeneres Show*, and the project was meant to be therapeutic. But because Mom hadn't worked on the project in over 10 years (it was something she'd started back when she lived in Upstate New York) and had lost the instructions, she had to improvise the process, and the whole thing put her in a bad mood, rather than relaxing her.

To make matters worse, Mia, Peanut and Rolz couldn't sit still for even a split second and would unravel all of her yarn and let it drop to the floor to roll underneath the couch where she couldn't reach it. After several days of this nonsense, the novelty finally wore off for them and they eventually got into the habit of settling in for a nap next to Mom rather than torturing her yarn. At this point, Mom's nerves started to calm down, and she began to appreciate their company and looked forward to the time they shared together.

I took the night shift and settled onto Mom's chest and hugged her neck with my big, furry paws while she watched TV with Dad. As she petted me, I could feel the stress of her body starting to ebb away with each of my comforting purrs telling her it would be okay. My plan must have worked because one day Mom was different. She got up from the couch in the middle of Ellen's show, something she never did before, and was actually smiling! I decided to follow her to see what was going on, and I saw that she was in her office, typing away at her computer like a possessed person. This made me very happy because I loved to hang out with her when she was at her computer – I jumped up to be near her in case she needed any advice from me and napped contentedly for the several hours she typed away as the warmth radiating from the computer soaked into my curled up body.

It turns out she'd had what she called an "epiphany moment," and it would forevermore change who she was. The afternoon she jumped up from the couch was sparked by watching Ellen do a segment about using a vision board to conceptualize her dream of being on the cover of Oprah Winfrey's "O" magazine, calling it her "O, Yes I Can," campaign. Mom had secretly been thinking about writing a heartfelt and humorous book about Zee and Zoey's love story and what it was like raising a family of kittens, but she didn't have the confidence to do it. She had always wanted to be a writer, and Ellen's positive attitude gave her the courage to get up off the couch and start typing the first chapter of what would eventually be called *The Chronicles of Zee & Zoey – A Journey of the Extraordinarily Ordinary* and that would be the impetus to changing not only Mom's life, but mine as well.

If Mom was at the computer, it was a sure thing bet I was too...

A Public Life

NATURALLY ALL THIS newfound inspiration kept Mom very busy, and any time she was writing her book I was right there by her side helping her. I was enjoying my role as the cat of an aspiring author, and life felt good again. Mom frequently paused to pet me while typing, and I was happy to provide her with as much insight and guidance as I could through my lulling purrs. We were best buddies, and I looked forward to our days together. How was I to know things were going to change again?

As I said, Mom and Dad always made sure we kitties had fresh water and food each and every day and got plenty of love, playtime, and snuggles, so we never thought to question that something was still amiss. How could we know having Mom and Dad stay home with us every day could mean something bad? We loved having Mom and Dad around, so I was quite shocked one morning when Mom hugged me with tears in her eyes and said, "Goodbye buddy, I'll see you later on tonight. Mama loves you. You be a good boy and take care of everyone."

Huh? I thought back to Bailey, Tosha, Kit, Bandit, and the others. "Goodbye" meant going to the Rainbow Bridge and never coming back. But Mom said she would see me later on that night and I knew she would never lie to me, so I wandered about the house for a bit after she left and finally settled on the bed she and Dad shared for a long nap, trying not to worry. I'll admit I had trouble sleeping and missed her like crazy, but sure enough, just like she said, early in the evening the front door opened and she was home. She fed all of us kitties dinner like she always did, and she and I snuggled on the couch after dinner like any other night, so it seemed like everything was back to normal and I was worrying for no reason.

The next day I woke up and the same thing happened – Mom left for the day and then came home later that night to feed us dinner and to snuggle with me on the couch. After a while I remembered that was how life used to be before the kittens were born. The only difference was both Mom and Dad would be gone during the day. I wasn't sure what was going on until I overhead Mom and Dad talking. They were both sad – they'd hoped to start a business together to help pay the bills, but it just didn't happen like they'd envisioned and they were forced to look for outside employment.

It seemed Mom had finally found a job, and even though it pained her to leave us all, she had to go so we had money to make sure we could still have a house, food, and clean litter. I really didn't like her leaving us, but I didn't want her to be even more upset by knowing that; not to mention, the thought of not having a home, food, or clean litter was appalling to me, so I rounded up the gang and told them we had to show Mom just how much we appreciated her going to work for us.

Now when she came home from work, all of us would be waiting by the door to greet her. We could hear her car a couple of blocks away so we always knew *exactly* when she would be home. Mom and Dad were amazed at our skill, that we were able to do this, but the truth is, we cats are not only intelligent, but we have a sixth sense and an incredible ability to hear sounds that might not be audible to humans.

She would barely have her foot in the door before all of us would rush at her – twenty-eight furry legs wove in and out of her human legs, nearly causing her to trip and fall, and we meowed a chorus of appreciation that she was home. She always thought we were saying, "Hurry up and feed us," but she was wrong. We were saying, "Hi Mom! Welcome home! We missed you!" Then we would tell her to hurry up and feed us – after all, we were hungry cats!

Since it was the reality of our life, we all got used to the new routine because we knew Mom didn't have a choice in the matter. I spent most of my time napping and also came out in the afternoon to spend some time with Dad, who had since found a job that let him work from home. He would pet me and we would chat for a while about our day – I would tell him about a lizard I was dreaming about and he would tell me about the clients he was working with (blah, blah, meow, meow), and after that I would go back and nap until Mom got home.

A couple of months later, Mom got even busier. She finally finished her book – her first one ever and she even self-published it all by herself! It was a gorgeous book filled with hundreds of amazing pictures Dad had taken of us felines, and the story was funny, sweet, touching, and inspiring. Not only did it chronicle the lives of Zee and Zoey, but it really captured the essence of how a cat's mind works and why we make such wonderful and cherished pets. There was even a special chapter devoted just to me (Chapter 3 called "A Cat in Bear's Clothing – Mr. Jazz"), and even though most of the book was not about me, I didn't mind. I was really proud of the story and didn't need to be the star of the show. I was never that kind of cat and was more than happy to hand the fame and glory to Zee and Zoey.

As a result of publishing the book, Mom had to do all the marketing, and she even put together a blog called *Zee & Zoey's Chronicle Connection* (subsequently renamed *Zee & Zoey's Cat Chronicles*) that continued to follow the daily trials and tribulations of not just Zee and Zoey, but Zee, Zoey, Mia, Peanut, Rolz, Harley, and me. She started traveling by herself a lot to attend events like blogging conferences and book signings, all while she was working a full-time job. Not to mention cooking, laundry, errands, and all the other stuff humans do. Thinking back on it all, I honestly didn't mind how hectic her life was because no matter what, Mom never, ever denied me attention if I asked for it, and I was really proud of what Mom had accomplished and always knew she loved me.

Not to mention, the life of a public cat had some great perks – even though Mom traveled sometimes, requiring her to pull out the dreaded suitcase that consequently meant she was going to leave us for a few days while Dad took care of us (which we hated – don't get me wrong, we didn't hate Dad, but we hated Mom leaving us because we missed her so much), when she came home, her suitcase was *always* magically filled with all kinds of great kitty toys and treats for us to enjoy. Being cats, naturally we initially ignored her upon her return to display our displeasure at her for abandoning us, but since the swag in her suitcase was sooooo darn tempting, we could only hold off for a few minutes before we were rifling through her bags like a bunch of seasoned TSA agents pawing for illicit catnip! Mom always laughed about that because she could only imagine what the real TSA agents thought she had in her suitcase since catnip looks so similar to you know what!

Having fun with some of the stuff Mom would bring home for us!

Mom also let us kitties help her with product reviews because we were constantly getting the newest and best cat stuff shipped to us to try out (the boxes they came in were always the best to play with in our opinion) so Mom could blog about it. No doubt we were spoiled to the max and living the life of pampered luxury. And even when Mom did blog, she included me in the process (some of the blog posts were even just about me). I either sat on the chair next to her in the office or napped by her computer while she was typing, and then when she was done for the day, every night, without fail, she sat on the couch with Dad to watch TV before we all went to bed. I snuggled on her chest and cradled her neck with my fuzzy paws, Harley would be in between Mom and Dad, and Zoey would be stretched out on Mom's legs. This was my all-time favorite part of the day, and I knew it was Mom's favorite part of the day, too.

When it was finally time for bed, I would follow her into the bedroom (along with Zee and Harley), and the minute she tucked herself in and turned on her side to sleep for the night, I draped my warm body over her middle. Even if it was uncomfortable for her, she never once complained and would never dream of disturbing me to move. Years ago it used to be a battle with Zee and me – we had a male testosterone kind of thing going on (so says Mom), and he and I got slightly competitive with each other as to who had primary rights to sleep next to Mom. Sometimes I got myself into such a tizzy that Mom actually had to shoo me off the bed to calm me down for a few minutes before I jumped back up and finally settled down for the night.

Now that I was older, I realized there was no need for games. Mom always let me sleep next to her, and once I understood that, there was no point in getting all worked up over it. And once Zee saw there was nothing to challenge, he stopped jumping up on the bed and that was that. Life was back on track and nothing much new happened. Harley still spent most of her time on the couch, and Mia, Peanut, and

Rolz were young adults now who acted much more calm and mature than in their early kitten days when they were constantly getting into everything.

And Zee and Zoey – well, they had settled into a quiet and loving relationship. We even had a new housemate Mom brought home unexpectedly from work one night. She had gone into a Pet Supermarket after work with the intention of buying us food like she always did, but instead she found herself hopelessly in love with a kitten in a cage, staring into the very depths of her soul, beckoning her to take him home, like some tragic Shakespearean poem.

His story was brief and simple – the only thing Mom knew was that he was about four months old and had been found abandoned by someone on the side of the road when he was just a tiny kitten. Mom's heart melted when she saw him, bringing her to tears, and all it took was one brief call to Dad for the okay, and he was brought to his new furever home with all of us. Ironically he looked like a combination of Zee and Zoey – he had a big, fluffy tail and a mane around his head like Zee and his coat was peppered with spots like Zoey! He was grey in color like Zee and actually looked more like what Mom and Dad had thought Zee and Zoey's kittens would look like than their actual kittens did!

Mom named him Kizmet, as in fate and destiny, but spelled with the letter "z" instead of "s" for the Zee and Zoey legacy. Kizmet was a special cat from the very beginning, and I remembered back in the deep recesses of my mind when my mother had told me about certain special cats being an "old soul." I knew at that very moment what she meant. Kizmet was different – he had such a sweet, kind, and caring heart – almost like he had been on this earth at some other time, and I never once felt any unease having him in the house. Actually, in many ways, he reminded me a lot of Kit, which is probably why it seemed like I felt I had already met him.

Life really was good – there were eight of us cats now, and I must say we all got along very well and loved one another dearly. We had plenty of windows to soak up the sun on and we also had an incredible backyard that Mom and Dad let us explore sometimes. The yard was fenced in and we were all well supervised when they took us out, but to us it seemed like an adventure in the great jungle, and we never tired of those special days.

There were also many times when all of us would converge on the bed in Mom and Dad's bedroom – first we would groom each other for a few minutes and then we would settle in for an all-day nap. We also had numerous cat condos, scratching posts, cat toys, pet beds, and everything else we could think of that would appeal to a cat. We never once went a day without food or loving, and because of Mom's blogging we were kind of famous in the cat world and had thousands of human and feline friends. I was very content to say the least, and I felt very, very blessed for my life.

So why was Mom looking at me differently tonight before we went to bed? Like something was wrong? The look was vaguely familiar, but I couldn't quite put my paw on it.

I was sensing that Mom was looking at me funny...

The Beginning of the End

THAT'S THE THING with life. It just keeps on going on around you until one day it sneaks up on you, and before you know it, you're a senior cat at age 15. We were both in the kitchen – Mom and me – and I saw her catch her breath. She didn't say anything, but her eyes told me volumes. Jazz is getting old, they said.

Kit. I flashed back. That was the look she used to give Kit when she would get all teary eyed looking at her. Her demeanor changed with me, more lingering glances, more "Hey buddy, how ya doing?" said to me.

Darn it, I thought to myself. I didn't think she'd noticed. I'd tried my best not to draw attention to myself and alarm her, but deep down I knew I wasn't kidding anyone. During the Easter holiday we had company, and I overheard them talking – my name was mentioned – something about me getting old. What? When did I become old? I still played with wadded-up balls of paper, didn't I? Or did I? I honestly couldn't remember any more.

Yeah, I was getting skinnier, drinking more water, and going to the litter box more. So what? Can't a cat lose a little weight without everyone making a big deal out of it? And maybe I just didn't feel like eating. And yeah, maybe I wasn't grooming myself as much as I used to, but seriously, at my age, who was I trying to impress? It's not like I had any special lady cat on the horizon that I was interested in. Sometimes Mom would get so consumed with what she was working on that maybe she would skip a shower here and there. No one gave her the third degree.

I couldn't deny it any longer – I was getting skinnier

And then it happened. Dad said to Mom, "Deb (that's what he called her), we need to think about taking Jazz to the vet." I saw Mom lower her eyes – she couldn't even look at Dad – and she said back in a shaky voice that she agreed. They both tried to reassure one another that it wasn't a big deal – just a routine checkup for me and to get some advice if necessary.

The call was made and the ordeal began. Mom no longer had that hateful plastic prison from years ago and instead had a beautiful cat carrier called a Sleepypod® that she used when she needed to take us kitties to the vet. It was one of the items I had given my personal stamp of approval on when Mom reviewed it on Zee and Zoey's blog, and I napped in it all the time because it was just that comfortable. It was round, perfect for a kitty to curl up in, with a soft, plush lining, and it had a domed, mesh lid that she could unzip and pet us through. When she picked me up to put me in it, I have to admit I didn't even put up much of a struggle like I would have years ago. Normally a good chase looking for me would have ensued, or at the very least, I would have scratched Mom as she tried to put me in the carrier. Much to my disbelief, I just didn't have the fight in me, and in some ways, I think I understood it was important I go.

When we got there, I was a very good boy according to Mom, Dad, and the vet. I was poked and prodded, and blood and X-rays were taken; yet I barely put up a fuss. Mom and Dad talked among themselves and the vet took lots of notes about me. My weight loss and increasing trips to the water bowl was of concern, but otherwise I was in good shape, so we had to wait for the results before any genuine plan of action (if necessary) would continue.

The vet came back several minutes later and said I didn't have diabetes, which could have been a possibility. It seemed I probably was in the stages of low-grade kidney failure, but the results weren't entirely conclusive. The most important thing at this point was to significantly bulk up my weight before we moved on. The humans talked for a few minutes about my condition and then the vet injected me with fluids and gave me a pill to stimulate my appetite – he did it with a practiced, casual ease that would suggest no alarm that anything was wrong with me and I instantly felt better.

Despite the brave front, Mom and Dad were visibly shaken over the whole ordeal, but they remained hopeful that whatever it was that ailed me could be fixed. And the good news was when I got home, I actually was hungry and I did start eating.

Declaring War

THE THING WITH FALSE HOPE is that sometimes it's the only way to get through the day. Mom and Dad were overjoyed I was eating something and would have preferred to live in a world of denial, but the truth was, I still wasn't eating a lot. Or I should say wasn't eating enough because back to the vet I had to go. Apparently the last time I was there I wasn't paying close enough attention to the conversation between Mom and Dad and the vet because I guess they agreed to bring me back if I wasn't eating up to the ridiculous standards the vet had set.

Two cans of food a day? Holy mackerel – what did they think I was, a dog? Surely a few dainty bites of food here and there would be enough to pacify them into thinking I was eating. Obviously I felt full or I would be eating more. *But no*, nobody was satisfied, and my foray into total humiliation began as I was once again put into the carrier and brought back to the vet for an appointment I hadn't requested. Blah, blah, talk, talk, notes, notes, and then I got infused with fluids again. This time a syringe came out. Something I was not at all familiar with and in case you don't know what it is, a syringe is a despicable and demeaning apparatus meant to shove food down a throat. In this case, unwanted food, and down my throat.

The vet showed Mom and Dad how to use the syringe and then stocked them up with cans of food that apparently had extra nutrients and super powers to bulk up my weight. He made it seem easy-peasy – just fill the syringe with food and presto like magic, inject it into your cat's mouth – your cat who won't put up a vicious fight, therefore allowing the disgusting and vile food to slide easily down its throat. Repeat this every day ad nauseam and voila, just like that, a brand new, happy and calm cat with a perfect weight! Okay, so maybe that's not what the vet said, but Mom and Dad put on a cautious pair of rose-colored glasses and that's what they pretended to hear.

Me in better days before my life become a nonstop battle with Mom to get me to eat

When we got home, however, the battle lines were drawn and the rose-colored glasses were quickly shattered. Mom put on her fighting face and that's when the war really began, which kind of sounds silly because on the surface it would seem Mom had an unfair advantage over me. Not that she's a big lady – she barely weighs as much as a bag of cat litter – but she was bigger than me and I guess she figured in my skinny and weakened state it would be easy to shove a syringe of food down my throat.

Well, wrong, wrong, wrong, and wrong again. I channeled every bit of strength I could muster, and it practically took an army to pry my jaws open. Mom needed Dad to hold me down, and I squirmed and scratched with such intensity that barely a morsel of food went down my throat. Most of it ended up smeared around my mouth, and it was the most humiliating and exhausting ordeal I'd ever gone through. And they seriously thought they could do this to me throughout the day to equal two cans of food? Not on my watch, I can assure you.

Not that they didn't try, and I don't like admitting this, but I started to resent Mom and really dreaded seeing her. Anytime she would come near me, I would run and hide from her. I knew it hurt her feelings – she cried a lot around me, and those times when she could catch me, she had to wrap me in a towel to keep me from scratching her. Most of the food she fed me ended up on the towel, her hands, and on the floor from me spitting it out – in other words, just about anywhere other than down my throat.

Sometimes she dipped her fingers into the mushy food and tried to shove it down my throat without the syringe, desperately trying to pry my jaw open to get me to eat – occasionally it worked and she got some food down me, but truly very little food ended up in me and certainly not enough to be bulking me up. She continued trying every brand of food under the sun to tempt me to eat as well as anything else she could think of, like baby food, turkey, and cheese, but it was clearly a losing battle. I didn't like Mom very much anymore and Dad wasn't much better. I just wished they would both leave me in peace, and I didn't care about anything anymore.

Showing my displeasure with Mom when she came looking for me...

Small Miracles

NATURALLY MY BEHAVIOR was alarming, and Mom and Dad instantly reacted (overreacted if you ask me) by bringing me to the vet. Dad happened to be traveling at the time, so Mom brought me alone. I was given a more thorough exam and this time they found some sort of aberration on my throat. Was it dangerous?

They weren't sure but even if it wasn't, that sure was a scary sounding word. Aberration. Wasn't there a nicer word to say something was on my throat? The vet went into a long and confusing litany as to what might, or might not be causing it. Mom just kept wringing her hands, and I could smell the fear and stress coming off her. Ironically, I felt calm. I wasn't in pain; I just wanted to be left alone and for all the tests, pokes, and prodding to stop.

To make matters worse, I knew from the suitcase in the bedroom that Mom had a trip to take in a couple of days, and she was already a basket case because of that. Dad had come home from his trip, and she wondered if she should cancel hers. I knew she didn't want to say it out loud, but I think she was afraid I was going to die while she was gone and that wracked her with pain and guilt. The trip was a conference to learn more ways to help other kitties as part of her blogging and advocacy issues, and she was really torn.

Me, I just wanted her to go and give me a break. I couldn't stand the syringe. I hated the food she was trying to shove down my throat, and I hated that she made me feel this way about her. Didn't she realize she was making it worse? I barely had any energy and spent most of my day stressed out, trying to hide from her, because she just wouldn't leave me alone.

Willing my thoughts to Mom for her to go and leave me alone

I loved her, but the whole thing was just so humiliating and confusing. Kit never told me about this part of it. She made it all seem so dignified and easy but it wasn't. I willed my thoughts to Mom.

"Mom," I said to her, "I promise I won't die. Please just go. Give me some time alone with Dad to collect myself. You'll see. Things will be better. I promise. I just need a break." I didn't know if what I told her was true, but I believed it to be so, and the promise I gave her gave me something to focus on other than not wanting to eat.

So with a heavy heart, Mom finally decided to go and packed her bags and off she went. She called Dad literally every other minute to check up on me and to see if Dad was forcing food down my throat like she did. She knew he hated doing it and worried Dad would give up and not even try. Dad finally got so frustrated with her that he told her to stop calling because her constant interruptions were just making it worse on everyone. He said he would try and asked that she please just leave him alone.

It was during all of this that the vet called. Mom was still at the conference and didn't hear her phone ring. He left a message that she could barely understand – something about what they found on my throat. She immediately called him back in a panic, but he was no longer in the office. She called Dad, almost unable to speak, her voice choked with tears, and he said he would call the vet for her to find out what the heck was going on.

I guess the vet needed to see me right away, so Dad put me in the carrier and off we went. As per usual, blah, blah, talk, talk, notes, notes, and then sub-fluids injected into me. Dad wasn't quite as calm and nice as Mom could be, and he and the vet kind of got into a heated discussion, but I understood why. Nobody really knew what was wrong with me and the bottom line was Dad just wanted an answer. Is there something to make Jazz better or not? That's all he wanted to know.

The vet told Dad, without spending thousands and thousands of dollars on tests that quite frankly might not determine anything conclusive, he didn't have a miracle answer and gave Dad the simple truth of it – just bring your cat home and love him as much as you can. Sometimes that's all you can do.

I wanted to jump up from the examining table and give him a big, furry hug. Finally, someone understood. It was getting closer to my time. I didn't want all the tests. I didn't want to have to ride in the car every week. I didn't want Mom stressing out anymore, and I didn't want syringes, feeding tubes, or anything else. I just wanted my peace and dignity, and once I finally heard someone say out loud that I might get it, my body instantly relaxed.

Dad told the vet he would talk to Mom, and when she got back from the conference they would decide what to do. When I got home and Dad let me out of the carrier, I felt like the weight of the world had been lifted from my worn out body. I jumped up for the first time in a long time to my favorite cat tree and even came out at dinner time to eat with the other cats on my own. Granted, I didn't eat a ton, but it was enough to warrant some pictures of me to be sent to Mom on her phone.

It wasn't a miracle, but it was close enough.

A Truce Is Made

AFTER WHAT SEEMED like an endless couple of months of torture, it appeared a truce was made. Dad and I bonded while Mom was away, and I started to relax a bit. I can't lie and say I was better, but I was content. I continued to eat small amounts on my own, and by the time Mom came home I was a changed cat. I felt happier than I had in ages and it was wonderful.

Mom understood the transition and finally listened to what I was saying to her. That's the thing with us cats – if you really take the time to understand our body language, you'll see that we're actually communicating to you. I was telling her that I accepted my fate and she needed to do the same. Enjoy the moments you have with me, I told her. Don't wallow in despair and anger. Celebrate my existence as it is and let nature take its course with me. When the time is right, I'll be ready to go and I want you to let me.

I can't say Mom always fully understood what I was saying. Sometimes she still tortured me, like stalking me to comb out my snarled fur that I no longer felt the desire to groom. She thought she was doing me a favor by clipping and combing the mats, but she wasn't. I hated it about as much as

I hated her shoving food down my throat, and eventually I was able to convince her to leave me alone (or should I say, my sharp claws and hissing convinced her to leave me alone) much as it pained her. To keep her at bay, I decided to distract her with eating, and I become obsessed with an eating pattern I'd begun to develop.

One of my favorite "leave me alone" places

In the course of Mom buying every food on the planet to try to placate me into eating, one of the things she bought was a cheap bag of dry kibble that probably didn't have the best nutritional ingredients possible. Now mind you, she'd tried every other nutrition-rich brand prior to that, trying her best to be a responsible pet parent, but I turned my nose up at everything. At this point, she didn't care. Her only goal was to get me to eat. I guess perhaps you humans would probably compare this bag of cat food to a McDonald's Happy Meal, and lo and behold, I loved it! So much so that every three or four hours I would stand in front of the kitchen pantry where our cat food was stashed and softly meow to Mom or Dad that I was hungry, and then one of them would hear me and stop what they were doing to give me a handful of the kibble to nibble on.

The kibble renewed my appetite, and I was willing to start eating some special canned food that through trial and error, Mom found I really liked, and that became my day. In the morning before she went to work, she would give me as much canned food as I would eat – she would always prompt me to eat more than I wanted, but I always remained firm in how much I could tolerate and stubbornly walked away when I was done. While she was at work, Dad would give me dry kibble snacks during the day, and at night I would eat dinner with the other cats. I would also get a kibble snack before bed. I had Mom and Dad very well trained with this routine.

I also started to snuggle on the couch at night with Mom again and put my paws around her neck like I used to. It was hard for her because I know she was doing her best not to be sad around me. She was used to a cat with silky, luxurious fur and a full body weight. I was a meager remnant of myself, but despite that, we both looked forward to this time and took it at face value. Nothing more, nothing less other than enjoying the moments we were given and I appreciated that gift from her more than anything.

All in all, life seemed relatively normal. Peanut, Zee, and Harley appreciated my morning breakfast routine because Mom let them lick the dish after I walked away, and Rolz became equally obsessed with my dry kibble addiction during the day and at snack time at night. Zoey, Mia, and Kizmet weren't hardwired to care as much about food, so they pretty much stayed out of the equation and let me be.

Mom wasn't completely thrilled with the others eating my food, but she was willing to give them a little bit here and there to keep them happy because if Mom is anything, she's fair. Even with all the extra time and effort she was giving me, she always tried to make sure she told the others how much she loved them and gave them as much attention and petting as possible. When we were on the couch and I was on Mom's chest, Dad would be next to her, Zoey on Mom's outstretched legs, and Harley would be in between all of us, just like always.

Treasured times on the couch with Mom, Zee, Harley, and Zoey

This routine went on for quite some time – for well over a month – but one morning Mom came to feed me breakfast, and she let out a feral-sounding scream after she bent down to pet me a good morning.

A Startling Discovery

I DON'T MEAN TO BE crude, but as I said, I wasn't up to par with my grooming habits. Mom did her best to help me out, but sometimes when I ate I got food on my chin and my body gave off a slight odor. My litter habits weren't so great now either, and as a result, Mom started putting pee pads in strategic places around the house because sometimes I just didn't feel like using the litter box. I always tried to get close to it, but that wasn't always easy, so sometimes Mom found pee puddles in unexpected places.

Thankfully Mom never made a fuss or made me feel embarrassed. She never, ever complained and never once did she make me feel like less of a mancat. We both understood my circumstances and had a silent agreement of not talking about it. I also drank a lot of water, so she understood my situation and just wanted to make my life as easy and comfortable as possible, for which I was grateful.

In any event, that morning she noticed an even stronger odor, like something rotting, but she didn't immediately connect the dots until she looked at me, and that is when she screamed. Underneath my neck was a huge, protruding bubble, the size of a golf ball, that was leaking a mucus-type liquid. Mom screamed, "Oh my God, Jazz" over and over, crying as she said it and ran off to the bedroom to wake up Dad. I just sat on the floor waiting for her to come back, dazed and confused by it all.

It took Mom a while to wake up Dad, and he really didn't understand what she was saying. Something about Jazz – have to go to the vet – now – emergency. Dad got up and took one look at me. I saw the concern in his eyes. No one was being tactful or polite anymore. They were scared that this would be the last day they would ever see me.

I was too confused myself to even understand what was going on. I don't think I was in pain, but I knew something bad was happening. Mom put me in the carrier and petted my head the whole way to the vet, not even bothering to stop crying for fear of upsetting me further. I honestly didn't mind her crying; it distracted me from what was going on and gave her something to do.

Our regular vet wasn't there, and Mom could barely speak to the receptionist. She choked out my symptoms, relatively incoherent, but her message was clear. I needed immediate attention. The vet who looked at me was a female human whom I'd never met before. She was nice enough, but because Mom and Dad were so worried about me, she put them on edge with all her questions. All they wanted was for me to be okay, but deep down they were terrified at what she would tell them.

With surprising evenness, she said I had an abscess and lanced it in seconds in front of Mom and Dad. All the liquid started to drain from the protrusion, and despite the temporary pinching feeling from the lance, I quickly felt much better. She didn't seem alarmed or surprised at all by my appearance, like she saw cats with golf ball sized protrusions on their neck every day of her life.

She gave me some pain medication as well as one of those horrific plastic cones to wear around my neck. She told Mom I would need a disinfecting compress several times a day on my neck along with more of the same pain medication I had just been given. Well, that sure was great news, and I couldn't wait to go home. But naturally, that was not the end of the conversation. All of a sudden she became very stern and told Mom and Dad they would have to make a decision soon because even though it might not seem like I was in pain, I might be hiding my feelings, because we cats have a tendency to do that.

She wasn't sure what caused the protrusion. It could have been something as simple as a small scratch that got infected or something more serious. Again, the same old conversation – we can do lengthy tests, blah, blah, scary talk, don't know, no guarantees, it's your decision, we can't tell you what to do, we can only recommend, and on and on.

I could feel Mom and Dad getting more and more confused and frustrated. We had already been there for hours, and all of us just wanted to go home. Finally Mom said to Dad, "Let's go. We can't make a decision right this second. We need a few days to think things over. The bottom line is we have a 15-year old cat that has lived a wonderful life. We obviously don't want him to be suffering, and we certainly don't want his remaining days to be devoid of any quality. We'll get back to you."

And so to my relief, Mom put me in the carrier and we went home. And believe it or not, as soon as Mom took me out of the carrier, I went to my dish for food. I still had the cone around my neck, and Mom saw that it made eating all but impossible so despite what the vet advised, she took it off me. I was so grateful for that kindness and ate as much as my thin body could take. Then I walked as best as my wobbly legs would allow me to my favorite cat condo next to the front door. I jumped up like I always did and curled up for a nice sun puddle nap, blessedly letting the warmth of the sun infuse my chilled and worn out body.

Enjoying a glorious nap in the afternoon sun

Letting Go

MOM WAS THE BEST. She took care of me day and night – all of my medicine, my special foods, my antiseptic wash, cleaning my face, giving me lots of fresh water, and combing me as much as I would allow. My wound was healing nicely with no further incident, and we were cautiously optimistic with my progress. That lasted for about two months until the day I decided I couldn't eat anymore, and we both knew it was over.

It happened to be a weekend, so Mom was home from work. She woke up to feed me like she normally did, but this time she couldn't coax a bite out of me. She immediately went into a panic and started opening can after can of wet food to see if I would try something. I just turned my face and hobbled to the cat tree in the dining room to get away from her.

Rather than leave me alone like I hoped she would, she came to me with one new concoction after another to try – tuna, milk, cream cheese, lunch meat – you name it, she tried it. During all of it she was sobbing out loud, saying my name and begging me to eat something. I didn't want to be so mean, but I refused it all and turned my back toward her.

Go away, that's all I could think. Just stop what you're doing and listen to what I'm telling you. It was tough love on my part, but I had to be brutal because she just wasn't listening anymore. She was at her wit's end, and in complete desperation she'd gotten out the syringe and was trying to shove food down my throat again! She was crying, and I gave it every ounce of strength I had left – I scratched her and then promptly threw up every measly bit of food she'd managed to get in me.

She just looked at me and that was it. She finally heard me. "Oh my God, buddy," she whispered to me. "I am so, so sorry. I love you so much, and I promise I won't do this to you anymore." She gently petted my head and stayed by my side, and I finally truly understood what Kit was trying to teach me all those years ago. Humans are just not capable of making the decision of letting us go on their own. We have to help give them the strength and courage to do it for us. We have to let them know we're tired and we just want to go, and they have to let us even though we know it will be the hardest thing they'll ever have to do.

Eventually Mom walked away, but it was with a sad resignation, and it hardly meant she left me alone. She checked on me constantly, bringing me water, which I was still willing to drink, and trying to see if by some miracle I wanted food. Sometimes she picked me up and brought me to the litter box since it was getting harder and harder for me to walk because my starving body was so weak and frail, but I usually stepped out of the box without doing anything.

I know Mom thought she was helping me, but I was a really private cat. I preferred to relieve myself at night when no one was watching me. I didn't like to go in the litter box any more – I used the pee pads Mom had on the floor for me and I just wanted my dignity to remain intact. Mom tried her best to understand my needs and be respectful, but I knew she was consumed with fear and despair.

In Mom's mind, I was this cat – a cat from years ago that was still young and healthy

I was her baby – her beloved and beautiful Mr. Jazz. I had been with her through thick and thin – 15 years was a lifetime of memories and it was killing her to know she would have to say goodbye to me soon. I knew she was praying for a miracle, that she would wake up one morning and I would be back to my old self, but she and I both knew that was not to be. As it was, I could barely communicate with her anymore. The world around me was becoming more of a blur, and the lack of food in my body was causing me to hallucinate. Sometimes I even forgot where I was and just stopped in my tracks to lie down.

I also started to nest, and for reasons Mom and Dad found hard to comprehend, I found solace lying on the floor of the room where Mom kept all her Zee/Zoey books and Dad kept his exercise equipment. I found a corner that suited me and lay under the cold and unyielding machinery. It was awkward for Mom to get to me, but she tried nonetheless and brought a blanket for me to sleep on rather than the hard floor. She assumed I liked the hard floor because it offered some sort of cooling relief to my body, and she was right. I would lie on the blanket for a couple of minutes, but I would get restless and move back under the exercise equipment.

During the day she checked up on me every couple of minutes until I finally convinced her she had to stop. Her hovering was making me nervous, and all I wanted to do was prepare my body for a peaceful journey to the new world waiting for me. I needed my personal space, and eventually she got my message and let me sleep, uninterrupted, for a few hours at a time.

Bedtime was her exception. No matter where I was at night, she would grab a pillow and two blankets – one blanket for her and one for me. She would gently pick me up and lay me on the blanket so I would be warm and comfortable, and then she would put her blanket next to mine so she could lie down next to me and put her arms around me. She would talk to me while gently petting my head, telling me it was okay to go when I was ready and that she loved me.

I let her do this. It was important for both of us but I couldn't do it all night. Sometimes the other cats would lie down with her, usually Harley and Kizmet, which was comforting for her. Eventually my body would become restless, and I would have to find my alone space. That was the hardest part for her – I knew she wanted to follow me and was worried she might not ever see me again, but she always let me go and reluctantly got up from the floor and went to bed, mentally exhausted.

One Last Gift

THE DAYS SINCE I last ate passed like years for Mom. Even though it had only been a few days, it seemed like a lifetime, and they were heavy with fear for her. When she had to go to work she could barely concentrate on anything but me. The first thing she did when she came home was look for me. At this point, I wasn't myself any longer. I was in transition, and my body was starting its slow descent into shutting down.

One night, just like any other night before Mom went to bed, she brought a blanket to lie down with me. Harley came with her, and this time rather than settling next to Mom, Harley put her body next to mine. Mom tried to shoo her away, thinking she might be bothering me, but Harley insisted on staying and put the girth of her body next to mine, almost willing her love and warmth into me.

Mom realized Harley was saying goodbye to her friend, so she let her stay. It was a very beautiful moment for all of us, and it gave me an opportunity to tell Harley it was okay – that I was okay with it all. I knew I was dying and I wasn't afraid. I told her I'd had a wonderful life – so many great memories – and it was up to her and the others to take care of Mom and Dad now.

Harley and I sharing a quiet moment

I knew when I was gone it would be hard for them, and it gave me an incredible sense of peace when Harley told me she understood and that I could leave without worry now. Harley and I had never really had any serious cat conversations before, but I knew I could trust her. She and I had been through the most together, and we had an unspoken bond of friendship born of mutual memories. Once we said our piece, I got up as I always did to find a place to rest my weary body as best I could, and Mom went to bed with her usual heavy heart.

On the morning of August 28, 2013, she woke up and couldn't find me. I heard her voice in the distance, frantically calling my name over and over – I knew she had to go to work and wanted to see me before she left so she could tell me she loved me, but I didn't have the strength to communicate where I was. I wanted to say, "Mom, I'm here." But I didn't have the energy, and I honestly didn't even know where I was. I was on my way to my final journey and was already approaching another dimension. I lay still as she continued to look for me.

Fraught with panic of the inevitable, Mom went into the bedroom to wake Dad. He was groggy, and in his mind he figured I was just hiding from Mom and her maddening insistence that she know where I was every minute of the day. But deep down he knew that wasn't the case at all and got out of bed to face the reality everyone wanted to postpone.

He looked high and low, calling my name over and over like Mom was, trying to be as upbeat as possible to keep Mom from falling apart with his own fears. He bent down and looked under the TV cabinet, saw my motionless body, and took a brief moment to collect himself before speaking.

"He's gone, Deb." He tried to say it without crying, but that was impossible, and he and Mom just held one another and cried.

Mom was immediately overwhelmed with grief, guilt, and profound sadness. "I wasn't there for him," she said. "Jazz died alone."

I could sense Mom felt she had let me down, that she hadn't done enough for me, and I prayed for just a few more moments on this earth to let her know I was okay – I understood her feelings and she was wrong. I loved her so much and didn't want those to be her final thoughts about me. I tried to regain my senses, and bless her little soul, somehow Peanut had heard my faint message.

"Mom, Dad, please," Peanut said. "Stop crying – don't you hear it? Jazz isn't ready to go. He's still with us and wants to talk to both of you."

Dad noticed Peanut's aggravation and bent down to pet her. "It's okay," he said. "I know that you loved Mr. Jazz, too."

"No," said Peanut with her body language. "Just listen – Jazz is trying to talk to you. He doesn't have much time left and he needs you to focus for a minute."

Dad continued to pet Peanut who became more persistent with her body language. "What's wrong, darling?" he asked her. "Peanut, are you trying to tell us something about Mr. Jazz?"

Dad and Peanut always had a special bond. She would sit on his shoulders while he was on the computer and let Dad cradle her in his arms like a baby all the time. He knew not to discount that she was telling him something so he bent down to look under the cabinet again.

"Oh my God, Deb, go get a towel," he said. "Jazz is still breathing. He's still with us, and you need to call work to tell them you won't be coming in today. Jazz is giving you his final gift – he wants you to be with him when he crosses the Rainbow Bridge."

It was true. I did want Mom with me. Even though I knew it would make her sad, I also knew I wanted her to take this journey with me. I wanted her to feel the warmth of my body one last time, and I also wanted to hear her soft voice tell me she loved me once more before I left.

Mom got a towel and Dad wrapped it around my frail body to carry me into the guest bedroom where the sun was shining through the windows in a glorious bath of comforting warmth. I honestly couldn't even see at this point and couldn't lift my head. I just sensed it all around me. The love, the serenity, the peace. It was so beautiful and it was exactly where I wanted to be.

The Final Hours

AS I LAY ON THE BED, Mom got herself situated around me. She grabbed a blanket I had helped her crochet a couple of years ago and found a comfortable pillow to put behind her back. She took off her shoes, turned the TV on so it was a low murmur of background noise, and settled herself next to me with the blanket tucked around her. I was on her left side and she laid her left hand on my still warm body to continuously pet me.

She stayed with me for hours and never let her hand leave me as she gently petted me and alternately spoke to me to tell me what a good boy I was and how much she loved me. Sometimes she would turn over to cradle her body into mine and just closed her eyes to talk to me telepathically. We did this on and off all day long until Mom had to get up for a few minutes to talk to Dad.

Even though I was still breathing, it was clear I was no longer with them and I heard bits and pieces of faint and fuzzy words – "what if he's in pain," "we don't know how much longer this will go on," "we have to do the right thing," "it's time," "we have to make the call."

Mom came back into the room and curled up next to me. This time she wasn't able to stay strong and just softly cried and cried. "Oh, Jazz, my buddy, I love you so, so much and I am so sorry. I don't want you to go, I don't want you to leave me."

I understood what she was saying. "But Mom," I said, "I'm already gone. You know that. Just let me go. It's okay."

Mom heard me and after a while she let herself stop crying. The day was quietly busy – Dad came in every hour or so to pet me and to tell me he loved me, and Kizmet and Harley spent the whole day with Mom and me on the bed. They were sad too and sensed Mom needed them around her. But despite how it might have seemed, it truly was one of the most beautiful and treasured days of my life. I was so loved and so cherished and it felt wonderful to know I could go in peace with nothing but great memories of a family I loved and adored that also loved and adored me.

The room was starting to close around me and I could feel my body leaving its physical being bit by bit. Mom wasn't holding me back and neither was Dad. "It's okay to let go, Jazz. It's okay, buddy. We're right here with you and we love you."

I was letting go – I could feel my body getting lighter and lighter, like I was floating. Mom... Dad... I... love..... you.... I was struggling, but only because I knew I had one final journey to make. I was so close to the Rainbow Bridge – so close to Kit, Bailey, Bandit, and the others. Mom and Dad were becoming fainter, and I thought I could hear Kit calling my name.

Dad came to pick me up one final time. He had emptied the large wicker basket we used to hold all our cat toys and gently lifted me from the bed, still wrapped in the warm towel, and laid me in the basket. I didn't stir – I was dreaming of Kit and couldn't wait to tell her how much I missed her and that she would be so proud of me. I did just what she wanted me to – I gave Mom and Dad the strength and courage to let me go and it felt wonderful. I felt joyous and wanted to meow like a young kitten again!

Dad carried me to the car and put the basket on Mom's lap as he drove me to the vet one last time. Mom cried again, but I wasn't mad at her. I understood. The tears were a combination of sadness, relief, and happiness that it would be over soon. Mom knew I had to go and she just wanted me to have my peace and dignity.

When we got there, the vet on call was already waiting for me. Mom and Dad followed her into a room that was dark except for the flickering of some beautiful candles that had been lit to give the room a serene and tranquil glow. It was just so touching and such a testament to the love everyone had for me. The vet didn't rush Mom and Dad. She gave them a private moment to talk to me one last time.

They both kept telling me it was okay, I could finally go now, and they loved me so much. I already knew that. I was already watching from above. The vet came back into the room, and Mom and Dad held each other and said it was time. They both petted me as the vet prepared me for my final journey. It was quick – I glanced back one final time. The vet was hugging Mom and comforting her. Mom and Dad were crying, but I was already on my way. I looked ahead and there she was – my buddy Kit – waiting for me just like she said she would be.

Without even giving it a second thought, I ran to her with the youthfulness of a cat half my age, my legs suddenly gloriously strong and muscled. My silky fur rippled gently from the wind of my energy as I raced to meet her, and tears of joy ran down my radiant, clear blue eyes as I meowed to her how happy I felt! She was right! Coming to the Rainbow Bridge didn't hurt at all and it was so, so beautiful! So much more so than I could have ever imagined, and my body felt so alive and free! All the pain I'd been saddled with for the past few months evaporated as if by magic and my mind and body were soaring as I took it all in. My senses exploded around me in a kaleidoscope of wonderment, and I was dizzy with excitement.

Kit looked at me, her eyes mirroring my own excitement, and she laughed like she had done with me so many times before when we shared our life back on earth with Mom and Dad. "Come with me, kid," she softly chuckled. "Bailey, Bandit, Shami, Tohsa, Whitney, Meadow, Hobo – all of us and so many more – we've all been waiting for you, and we have so much to share with you! Welcome to the Rainbow Bridge, your true furever home where pain and sadness no longer exist and every day is a day filled with love, peace, friends, family, and goodness."

My final blessed moments with Mom, Kizmet, and Harley

Rebirth and a Book Is Born

WHEN MOM AND DAD got home, it was surreal. Mom was in stunned silence and walked around the house in numbed disbelief. Everywhere she looked, she saw me. The house looked like a cat infirmary – there were syringes, pills, cans of food, pee pads, antiseptic, and everything else you can think of to prolong my life in every nook and cranny. She immediately began to remove the most obvious traces of my convalescence out of her sight to lessen the jarring punch in the gut she felt seeing these painful reminders of me, and she could barely look at the guest bedroom, the last place she had seen me alive in the house.

But the thing was, I was 15 years old and she had been preparing mentally for my death for months. Not that it made it better or easier, it didn't, but she'd been saying goodbye to me for ages. She had work, she had a blog, she had Dad, and she had the other cats and her friends and family. Life couldn't just stop because I wasn't around, but despite all that, letting me go hurt her deeply and it wasn't easy.

Being the cats of an award-winning blogger, most of what Zee, Zoey, Harley, Mia, Peanut, Rolz, Kizmet, and I did was an open book. Mom would blog about the big and small things we did with her typical honesty and humor, and she constantly shared the great pictures Dad took of us all the time. I didn't care for the fanfare as much as Zee, Zoey, and the others, but the fact was, in the cat blogging social world, a lot of people and cats knew who I was. What they didn't know, however, was that I'd been slowly dying for months. With the exception of a select few who had an idea of what was going on, Mom tended to my condition with privacy, and after I crossed the Rainbow Bridge, she didn't immediately share the news on Zee and Zoey's blog or other social platforms.

She just couldn't. She didn't want to talk about how empty her heart felt when she fed Harley, Zee, Zoey, Mia, Peanut, Rolz, and Kizmet dinner and my bowl remained untouched. She didn't want to talk about how hard it was to see my specially designated kibble in the pantry, never to be eaten by me again. She didn't want to talk about how she could never again wear the clothes she had on the day I crossed the Bridge because the sight of them hurt her too much or that she couldn't go in the guest bedroom because it pained her too deeply to be in the room where she had last seen me. She didn't want to talk about how hard it was to get used to the fact that I was no longer part of the "cat head count" to say goodbye to before she went to work in the morning, and she especially didn't want to talk about the guilt she felt that maybe she didn't do enough to help me – she battled in her mind over and over with the "what ifs." The truth was, she was in denial about my death and I think she felt that if she didn't talk about it, then maybe I really hadn't gone.

But Mom is a writer at heart, and for her, sometimes writing is the only way to express her feelings, so a few days after I was gone, she finally found the resolve to write about letting me go. She shared the post on Zee and Zoey's blog along with the last picture of me ever taken. It was the picture I shared a few pages ago in this book, of me with Mom, Kizmet, and Harley. Kizmet and Harley were lying by Mom's feet and I was on the bed, slowly preparing for my journey to the Rainbow Bridge. Mom had her arms around me, hugging me, and even though it was an incredibly private moment, Mom let Dad take the picture because somehow it just seemed right.

The post came from Mom's heart and was aptly titled "A Tribute to Mr. Jazz – The Dignity of Life and Death and Finding the Beauty in Letting Go." It was touching, sad, reflective, and beautiful, and the reaction she got from her readers was overwhelming – not only did friends and family offer their condolences, kindness, and support, but so did perfect strangers who felt comfortable enough to share their own stories about their beloved pets that had crossed the Bridge.

That was when she realized my tribute post was not only important to helping her process her own grief, but it was an important outlet for those people who had experienced similar feelings of letting go of a pet who needed a place to express their own grief. A while after that, Mom knew she wanted to share my story. Not so much because she thought my story was that unique because truth be told, I really didn't live an extraordinary life – I was always a cat with simple needs and as I told you from the very beginning, those needs were always fulfilled.

I didn't live on the streets like Kit did, I wasn't abandoned like Harley and Kizmet had been. I'd never been in an airplane like Zeuss Catt, and I didn't have a grand love story like Zee and Zoey. I didn't knock things off the kitchen counter and break them like Zee, and I didn't climb up curtains like Zoey used to do. I'd never been scolded for being naughty like Mia, Peanut, and Rolz used to be when they were kittens, and I never wanted to escape out the back door to explore the yard like Kit tried to do.

My life was a wonderfully ordinary one filled with the typical highs and lows that just about anyone who has ever loved a cat can relate to. Because of that, Mom knew my story would resonate with a wide range of people who could take comfort that they weren't alone in the vast array of emotions they felt when having to let a pet go – from sadness, to anger, to despair, to guilt, and everything in between.

It was at that point I knew the story had to come from me and that my mother had been right all along – I was a special cat who did have a lesson to teach, but ironically it was through my death that I finally understood what it was. It needed to be the simple message to let our beloved human guardians know that we pets are grateful for the love, life, and companionship you give us and that despite what you might think, we don't hold a grudge or get angry with you if you have to make the difficult decision to let us go. We are hardwired from birth to know our time on earth with you is fleeting and borrowed in the scheme of your life span and we instinctively know to live in the joy of the present moment as a result of that.

The simple truth is that we pets don't live in the past, we don't live in regret, and we don't care about the surface realities that you might, such as what color skin you have, what religion you believe in, or what your sexual orientation is. We don't care about your income, if you have a college degree or not, or what kind of car you drive. We love our humans unconditionally, without prejudice or judgment, and all we ask is that you love us back in return and keep us safe, warm, healthy, and fed. So for me, personally, I have no regrets – I did live a long and full life – with each and every day filled with good food and treats, clean litter, lots of scratching posts to sharpen my claws on, endless wadded-up paper balls to bat at, warm laps to nap on, the revolving companionship of my fellow feline (and canine) family, and so many loving caresses and tender words from my humans.

I couldn't possibly ask for a better life, and I am so grateful Mom and Dad's deep love of me gave them the strength and courage to let me go, rather than to let me linger on and suffer because they couldn't bear to lose me. I know they would have preferred I died peacefully in my sleep so they wouldn't have had to make the painful decision to help me cross the Bridge, but because that was not meant to be, I am so proud of them for putting my needs ahead of theirs, even though I knew my passing would cause them immense pain and grief after I was gone as they mourned me. I look back with nothing but a sense of peace, knowing they will forever have me in their hearts, and I am joyous that the weight and burden of my dying days has been lifted from them and me.

All I ask of those of you reading my story is that you try to remember that life is finite. Love, treasure, and appreciate what you have in your lives as if it might be your last day because it very well might be. And when you lose a beloved pet like me, don't be closed minded, afraid to feel love again – open your hearts and homes when the time is right to another pet who needs a furever home because there are so, so many animals in shelters who deserve a chance for a happy life. I promise it will not dilute the love you had for us, quite the opposite – it will fill our hearts with joy knowing you have given another creature a chance to love you the same way we did.

Peace out all – until we meet again…

RIP Mr. Jazz – gone but never forgotten…

Epilogue

I KNOW I'M SUPPOSED to be gone, but I'm still here. Not here as in having my remains brought home in a pretty wooden box that sits on the TV stand or in the physical sense where Mom and Dad can actually pet me and feel the silk of my fur, but in the spiritual sense. As time has passed, my visits have lessened and maybe by the time this book is published I'll be completely gone, but after I met up with Kit I had a nagging feeling that even though the Bridge was incredible and I felt truly happy, I couldn't completely cross it because I was still needed for something.

I didn't initially know what it all meant, and at first I was hesitant to come back at all. My final moments with Mom and Dad had been so beautiful so I wasn't completely sure it was a good idea – I didn't want to make their grieving process even more difficult by prolonging my stay – so my appearances were very fleeting and random in the beginning. I also wasn't sure how it worked – I could see them, but could they see me? I had a strong hunch Mom saw me a few times, but because I hadn't been gone that long, I was thinking she probably just thought it was her imagination, willing me back to life.

I felt like I needed to know if she could really see me, so I decided to establish my presence with her in a more concrete sense, and one day I became bolder, standing a few feet away from her in the hallway to watch her. She was on the couch watching TV with Zoey on her legs and Harley by her side, just like any other night, other than that I was no longer sitting on her chest. She looked up and stared right at me, and this time I was certain she knew it wasn't her imagination. I really wanted to come and sit with her like old times, but even though she remained calm at seeing me, I thought that might be too much for her to handle in one night, so I decided to pursue our paranormal relationship in a more gradual fashion.

I thought back to bedtime which had always been our extra-special time together. Like clockwork, I would follow her into the bedroom and wait until she was settled into the bed for the night – eventually she would turn over on her side to sleep and that's when I would drape my Ragdoll body over her midsection (if you will recall, that's one of the characteristics of the Ragdoll breed – our tendency to relax and go limp). I loved to feel the warmth from her body, and the curve of her shape felt as if it was custom-made just for me. She used to reach out throughout the night to pet me in loving reassurance, so I felt starting here to make my presence known would be the gentlest way to let her know I was still with her.

I also felt by taking it slow that it would give me time to figure out my spiritual destiny with her, so at first I slept at the end of the bed on her feet. I knew she felt me, and I started there because I didn't want to overwhelm her with memories of me sleeping on her side right away. Each night I moved a bit closer, and eventually I was able to channel myself into Zee so that he found himself draped across Mom's body one night without knowing how or why he felt compelled to do it. I just felt it was the right way to handle things and there was no jealousy on my part – Mom relaxed with Zee on her body, and I knew she understood the transition was my doing.

And all the drawers I used to open – I also opened them on occasion to let Mom know I was thinking of her. Sometimes she woke up to find the drawer next to her bed pulled open and it was only that drawer – I left all the other drawers alone so they could be opened by Rolz who has taken up this habit since my passing. But opening drawers was not what it was supposed to be about either. I felt that my visitations had a greater purpose, but I still didn't know what they were.

I think in many ways Mom felt there was a greater purpose as well, but because she didn't know what it was, she sometimes felt guilty that I was still visiting her – she wondered if her grief and sadness were keeping me from crossing the Bridge, leaving me in a state of spiritual limbo because she couldn't fully let me go. I know she'd tried, but the truth was she hadn't done too well with mourning my passing – months had gone by and she remained in denial, and because of the pressures of life, work, and everything else, she had all sorts of excuses and reasons to never really give herself the time to just cry, deal with the reality of my passing, and let me go.

While I could understand her thinking, that was not actually the case. It made me sad that she was having trouble letting me go but that wasn't what was keeping me around in spiritual form. Eventually it all became clear – Mom was not doing so well. She and Dad had been going through a lot of really difficult situations of late and neither of them was in good shape emotionally. Since my passing, they'd lost a dear friend to cancer and Dad was unemployed again. They both were feeling lost, and during all of this emotional upheaval Mom was getting ready to go to a pet expo in Orlando for blogging and cat advocacy reasons (the Global Pet Expo). Rather than being excited about it, she wondered why she was even bothering to go. Nothing seemed to matter to her anymore, and she was having trouble connecting the dots about her future.

Since the expo was only about three hours away from home, Dad was going to be attending with Mom, meeting her cat writing friends for the first time, and they were going to visit Dad's mom who lived only an hour away after that. But Mom was feeling despondent and seriously questioning if they should even go, compelling me to do something I'd never done before – I came to visit her while she was in her office getting ready for the expo. She was on the floor with Rolz – he was sitting next to her while she was putting some marketing materials together – and I stood in the doorway and looked her straight in the eyes, willing her to see me.

Thankfully, she looked up from what she was doing, and her eyes locked with mine. Knowing I had something to say to her, she listened as I communicated in the simplest of terms that she needed to go to the expo. I just felt deep inside me that there was a reason she needed to go and for the first time ever since my death, when she came to sit on the couch that night, I came and sat on her chest like old times without worrying about spooking her. She felt the weight of my body on hers and instinctively reached out her hand to pet me. It was then that I knew she had heard my message, and we both sat on the couch feeling at ease for the first time in ages. I still didn't know what the expo would bring, but I remained confident all would become clear soon enough so I could finally cross the Bridge in peace.

The next day they left for the expo – Dad got to meet some of Mom's friends, and they had a full two days of appointments meeting with pet companies to learn about all sorts of wonderful new products to make the lives of pets happier and healthier. It was a much-needed distraction for both of them, and Mom was looking forward to blogging about their experience when she got back home. Dad took all sorts of great pictures, but when all was said and done, there really were no great lessons to learn so Mom put my visitation out of her mind. Was I wrong in my premonition? I didn't think so, but even I was beginning to worry that maybe I was off track. That was until the last day of the expo, right before they were getting ready to leave the event to go spend the night with Dad's mom.

Mom had one last appointment with the sales team at Imperial Cat – a company that makes really cool cat scratching posts. When she got to the booth, the person she was supposed to meet with was not there because of some sort of time mix-up so Mom and Dad decided to call it a day and leave early. That was until an orange kitten with a white bib and mittens caught their attention. She'd been given the name "Empress" and looked to be a Maine Coon (Dad's favorite if you recall), and she stole Mom and Dad's heart the second they set eyes on her.

She was a stray kitten that had apparently found her way into a barn of a farm owned by a couple in the Orlando area. As the couple already had their hands full with other rescue cats, dogs, horses, and birds, they couldn't care for the kitten and called a local organization, Florida Little Dog Rescue of Saint Cloud, to help them find a home for her. Somehow the rescue group hooked up with someone at the expo with the idea to showcase her in hopes that someone would be interested in adopting her, which is how she ended up at the Imperial Cat booth. As Mom and Dad didn't know her back story at this point, they had no idea if she would end up living in a shelter the rest of her life or, worse yet, if she would be euthanized if no one adopted her.

Plucky, bold, confident, sassy, adorable, and charming are the words that came to mind, and Mom and Dad were shocked to find out she didn't have a line a mile long waiting to adopt her. Not a single person had stepped up to provide her with a furever home, and it was unbelievable to them to think she might have to live her life in a shelter or worse. She was absolutely stunning, and Dad told Mom he wanted to bring her home. Mom wasn't as sure about it as him. First of all, she was still mourning me – I'd only been gone seven months and she didn't feel she was ready for another cat in her life right now. Secondly, they had nothing with them to transport a kitten back home, and thirdly, Dad's mom was not a cat person – how were they going to bring a kitten into her house for an overnight stay?

Do I need to have you read the first 25 chapters of this book again? Of course you know it was a losing battle and even Mom knew the minute she laid eyes on that ginger princess that they were about to adopt another cat. I can assure you, I knew then and there why my spiritual presence was needed. This little girl was meant to be, and I was the gateway to bringing her to Mom and Dad. Fate, destiny, kismet – call it what you want, but when I came to visit Mom that night while she was in her office, I knew she had to go to the expo, and it all finally made sense – another cat in need was about to find its furever home.

My namesake, Jazmine. It wasn't hard to understand why Mom and Dad fell in love with this precious little girl...

Mom and Dad ended up getting all sorts of cat stuff donated from several pet companies exhibiting at the expo so they could safely bring the kitten home – toys, food, litter, a cat carrier, a litter box, and so much more. She survived her stay with Dad's mom with flying colors (actually even charming her with her bewitching personality and adorableness) and when they finally got her home, she spent her first acclimation week in the room where I had spent my final moments before being brought to the vet to cross the Bridge.

Kizmet broke protocol by barging into her room the first day she arrived, and he instantly fell deeply in love with her, just as Zee had with Zoey. At this point, she still didn't have a name – Mom and Dad didn't want to call her Empress, the name she was given at the expo. They knew they would be picking out their own special name for her, and it came to Mom out of the blue one day as she was sitting on the very bed I'd shared with her on my last day on this earth – Jazmine.

Yes, it was perfect – a tribute to my name and memory by using the letter "z" in the name as opposed to the traditional spelling, Jasmine. And even more fitting, little Miss Jazmine likes to play with wadded-up balls of paper like I did and she loves to snuggle on the couch with Mom and Dad at the end of the night. Much as Mom and Dad still miss me, she has brought an incredible joy, youth, and exuberance into the house, and I take no offense to it whatsoever. Quite the contrary, I take great pleasure in knowing another cat in this world will live a life filled with love, happiness, and comfort the way I did. As I have said all along, I promise you that is the greatest legacy you can give a pet that has crossed the Bridge and it felt good to know there was finally a healthy peace and closure to my death.

And most extraordinary, in helping me write my story, Mom went through some old paperwork of mine to confirm exactly when she had gotten me. Because I wasn't purchased for my lineage, but rather because she wanted me as a beloved pet, Mom had filed my birth papers right away without looking at them or giving them a second thought. When she pulled them out of the folder she was shocked at what she saw – my mother's name was Jazzy Jasmine! In all my years of life, I'd never known I had the same first name as my mother and neither did Mom. Then, to see the Jasmine connection – wow, just incredible! Perhaps not earth-shattering news in the scheme of things, but to Mom and me, it was a sign that all of it was meant to be and my mother was right – she knew all along how special I was and that once I met my one true love human, we would "forevermore have an irrevocable bond together that would transcend the likes of this world and beyond."

Fifteen wonderful shared years together in the past, a spiritual relationship that keeps us connected in the present and an eventual future to look forward to where we will live in eternity in a glorious place known as the Rainbow Bridge – she and I will always be together and that is perhaps the greatest gift of all.

Memoriam

AS THE HUMAN MOM to Mr. Jazz, I graciously thank him for sharing his story with such honesty, humor, insight, and wisdom. His memory will forever remain in my heart, and not a day that goes by that I don't miss him and think about him. In helping him share his story, I have finally come to greater terms with his death – I have sobbed gut-wrenching buckets on many a day, reliving his death over and over through my writing, but I have also been given the privilege of reliving all the wonderful moments of his life. All in all, I think the writing process has been therapeutic, and as a result, I have finally been given the sense of peace and closure I so desperately needed.

Jazz is gone and is not coming back. But he remains immortalized, not only in my heart, but through this book, Zee and Zoey's blog and book, Facebook, Pinterest, and other social platforms, as well as through the countless photographs I have of him. His ashes sit in a beautiful wooden box adorned with his picture on our TV armoire where he rests with Bandit and Bailey – two of his buddies who were also cremated – and I am grateful he could finally cross the Bridge without worrying about my well-being.

Jazmine has come to help fill the void in our hearts with her larger-than-life personality and Kizmet, despite his young age, has stepped up to be quite the wise mentor and teacher like Jazz was. Life was moving on for us – certainly not without its pain and heartache, as I have to admit Dan and I have been on a very long and difficult journey of late – but as the eternal bright spot, we have the love and companionship of our cats, and even the darkest of days has a silver lining when you put it in that perspective. I thought Jazz's book was done and the proverbial "The End" could be penned.

One can never predict the future however, and sometimes we are taught brutal lessons that come out of nowhere that are entirely unfair and difficult to comprehend – especially when it comes to the loss of a beloved pet to completely unexpected circumstances. This book was long written in my mind and the story was finished. But fate intended the story to have a different ending – one I never in my wildest dreams could have imagined and one I never would have wanted.

We had been treating Harley for symptoms of asthma that had cropped up. It was a new development for her, and she was taking medication to help with her breathing, which seemed to help her feel better. I was glad to be able to help her on her road to managed recovery. About a week in, she started to stop eating, and thinking back to Jazz, I immediately took her to the vet. She had lost some weight, so the vet gave her fluids to hydrate her and a B12 injection to stimulate her appetite. Pretty standard stuff.

I took her home with the assumption all was going to be well, and I brought her into my office so I could keep an eye on her and shut the door. Zoey tends to get a bit uppity whenever one of the other cats comes home from the vet, and I didn't want her growling or hissing at Harley. I went in about five minutes later to check on her and to my horror, saw her on the floor in the grips of a severe epileptic seizure.

Dan was home, and we immediately took her back to the vet – the seizure lasted the entire car ride and was shocking to witness in its intensity. This was something that had never happened to her before, and the remainder of the story is far too painful for me to retell. I am not certain I will ever be able to share it in detail. All I know is that my Harley, my sweet girl who didn't have a mean bone in her body, had to be put down to cross the Bridge at only ten years of age.

There was no warning, no grace period like we had with Jazz whereby Dan and I got to say goodbye to him and prepare ourselves for the inevitable. When it came to crossing Harley to the Bridge, we were given but a few brief minutes. It was not a beautiful Hallmark moment, and there was no pretty pink bow to tie up the loose ends in a poignant and touching package so we could put our minds at ease as we remembered her. It was an unspeakably awful moment that cut to the very core of my heart, scarring my very existence.

I share this with you not to upset you, but because Mr. Jazz wanted his story to be a source of comfort and realism for those who have lost a pet, and the truth is, not all deaths make sense or are fair or have peaceful, fairy tale endings. The loss of Harley and the profound sadness I am struggling to deal with is the pain that so many others can relate to who have gone through similar circumstances. The simple message is this – whether it's a pet who has lived a long and full life that died peacefully of old age in its sleep, a pet that died as a result of a chronic illness, a pet that was unexpectedly hit by a car, an animal that didn't make it through birth, a pet that died for reasons unknown, an animal unjustly euthanized in a shelter, or a pet that was lost, never to be found again which is also like a death in many ways, the grieving process we as individuals go through as a result of their death is completely unique each and every time, and Jazz wanted to honor and respect those differences in his story.

There is no doubt my loss of Harley is far too soon to reconcile right now – I lost her a mere 10 months after Jazz crossed, and as I write this, I am still deep in the throes of fluctuating stages of anger, guilt, and denial. Sleeping is the worst for me – I am left alone at night to struggle with the demons that invade my thoughts as I replay her death over and over in my mind. I had to make the instantaneous decision to let her go – it wasn't supposed to be her time – I must have missed something that caused her to have her seizure – I killed her. I know in the far recesses of my mind that's not true. I loved her dearly and would have done anything for her – clearly I didn't know something like this would happen, but I can't help but feel that I am responsible. That I did this to her. That I killed my cat.

It's just too much power and responsibility to hold in one's hands when a pet has to leave us too quickly – a vet having to ask your permission to let a pet go, right there on the spot, and you giving them the go ahead to let it happen. But we can't let someone we love suffer, and she was suffering. That much I knew, and I had to let her go. I had no choice, and as a result of the emotional consequences I bear, it has left me detached from a life that continues on with alarming regularity as I struggle to come to grips with the reality of the situation.

I am forced to live like nothing bad has happened because I have to get up every morning and get on with the routine of my life – I drive past the vet's office every day because it's on my way to work, and I have to pretend that wasn't the last place I saw Harley alive. I have to open the credit card statement that clearly documents Harley's last day on earth, and I have to live through the normalcy of it all in the midst of my pain. Television commercials blare at me with obscene loudness, screaming at me to buy inane products I have no use for, and the radio jars my nerves when I listen to it with a pop song with the insipid lyrics "I like it better when we're wasted."

Probably the hardest part is that I still see her everywhere, and I have to deal with that as well. Not in the spiritual sense like I do with Jazz, but through the imagery of my mind. I can't let her go, and she haunts my every waking moment. I know it's psychological – I'm clearly in denial and until I make peace with her crossing, I am my own worst enemy. But right now that's how it is – I've received sympathy cards I can't open yet, I have emails people have been kind enough to send me that I can barely respond to, I've received an overwhelming outpouring of love and support on Zee and Zoey's blog that has been difficult for me to acknowledge, and Harley's ashes sit next to Mr. Jazz in a pretty and functional box that I can't even look at.

And I'm certainly not alone in my grieving – clearly Dan mourns the loss of his feline companion, and Zee, Zoey, Mia, Peanut, Rolz, Kizmet, and Jazmine are also feeling the loss of their friend and I'm certain they're grieving too. I know this because the first week after Harley's passing they lay on the rug in my office, only a few feet from where Harley had her seizure, as if to pay respect to her. They have since moved back to their regular napping hangouts with the exception of Kizmet, who barely moves from his spot on the rug.

Not only do they grieve, but they are also highly sensitive and intuitive and don't like to see the humans they love hurting. I was told this in no uncertain terms by Kizmet a week after Harley had passed. We were on the couch watching TV – Jazmine was amusing herself with a DaBird toy she had dismembered and the rest of the gang was hanging out within eye range. Out of the blue, Kizmet bounded onto the couch – I was lying on my side, mentally worn out and exhausted, with my head on a pillow. He came up to me with complete intention – pressing his nose firmly into mine to tell me he was there for me and he understood my grief. He then tucked himself into the bend of my belly as closely as he could so I could wrap my arms around him and cradle him. He stayed with me for several minutes, and it was truly a blessed and profound gesture of love and caring from him.

In the midst of my internal grief, his love has helped me immensely and was also a gentle reminder that it's not fair to overburden our remaining pets with our grief, so I continue on with regularity to groom, feed, snuggle, and play with them so they know how important they are to me. I still find it hard to allow myself the courtesy of smiles or laughter, almost as if it's a betrayal to Harley's memory if I give in to feeling some sort of happiness, and sometimes I question it all – I want desperately to believe she's in a better place and she truly is celebrating in a Rainbow Bridge filled with her old pals and it's peaceful and beautiful. I really don't know, but without that reassurance, I have to ask myself, what do we have?

How were we to know at that time that this would be
the last picture taken of our darling Harley?

As if to answer my question, I got the most amazing visit a few days after Harley's crossing. I woke up to find the drawer next to my bed was opened. I knew Rolz could open drawers, but this was the drawer Jazz always opened. I hadn't seen Jazz since he came to me to bring me the message that I needed to go to the Global Pet Expo, so I figured he had finally fully crossed the Bridge. Was he back to tell me something or was it just a weird fluke?

I put it out of my mind and got up to take a shower – when I was done, Jazz was waiting for me in the bedroom – in the exact spot where Harley had lain with him the last night he was with us before he died. He looked at me for several moments, locking his eyes with mine, and I am positive he told me that Harley had arrived and was safely with him. He was telling me to be kind to myself – to let me know Harley loved me and understood my pain and grief but I had to stop beating myself up – she knew it wasn't my fault she had to cross the Bridge – just like with Bailey, sometimes things happen for reasons we'll never understand – and she also knew she was loved and cherished and lived a wonderful life for the ten years she was blessed with.

He also caused me to stop and reflect. When we bring a pet into our home and heart, we know that ultimately they will leave us and we don't have control over the when, where, how, or why. Should we then not have a pet because we don't want to be hurt when they are gone, or in the long run, does the happiness they bring us outweigh the pain? I realized then and there that even though I was in excruciating mental pain at Harley's loss, the love, joy, companionship, and comfort she brought me while she was physically with me was worth it. Every single minute that I was blessed to have with her was worth it and my life was made all the better for having her be a part of it. The memories of good times can never be taken away from me – and that's the ultimate message Jazz taught me.

I am grateful for that reminder, and I'm trying as best I can to work through the pain I'm feeling at the loss of Harley. Our pets love us unconditionally and despite how it might feel to me at the moment, I know Harley bears no grudge with me. I also see now that Jazz will forever be connected to me – he and I share a paranormal bond and I no longer question his purpose. I now take his visits at face value and thank him for taking my Harley under his wise and gentle angel wings. Life remains a journey – what's in store for us in the afterlife, none of us really knows. All we can do is be true to the life we live – appreciate the moments we have – and hope whatever awaits us is indeed filled with the happy wags, barks, meows, and purrs of our beloved and cherished companions.

Family Scrapbook

Sweet Bailey

My best friend, Kit

Rough and tough, Bandit

Joe's 12th birthday

Christmas 2002 with Mom

Chris turns 15

Dinnertime with Mia, Peanut, Rolz, Harley, Zoey, and Zee

I always loved opening drawers

Playtime with Dad and Harley

Naptime with Zee, Rolz, Mia,
Zoey, Peanut, and Harley

All of
us
helping
Mom
write

A leopard
inspired
nap!

Guide to Coping with Pet Loss

WHETHER YOU HAVE GRIEVED the loss of many pets in your life or are experiencing it for the first time or if you have a beloved pet with an eminent death you'll have to face soon, there is no quick and easy ten-step guide with a magical formula to healing the heart. With each death comes a unique set of circumstances, and the grieving process is a highly individual experience with no rules or timeframes as to how you should, or should not, process the pain.

First and foremost, because each situation is so personally unique, the grieving you go through will be based on the individual relationship you shared with your pet. Some pets hold a stronger bond in our hearts than others, some pets have been with us longer than others, some deaths are expected, and some are brutal tragedies that come out of nowhere – all of these circumstances will affect the intensity and duration of your pain. This holds true even if more than one person has a relationship with the pet that died – each person will mourn the loss differently.

Our own personal life is also a factor in how we grieve – maybe you're someone who doesn't have a social outlet and your pet is your only friend or maybe the animal was a loyal and devoted worker companion that was a necessary part of your daily living routine. Or maybe the pet was an integral part of a family and was the best friend to a child. All of these scenarios, and countless more, affect our feelings and the ways in which we grieve.

Given the intense bond most of us share with our pets, it's natural to go through a range of emotions such as despair, anger, guilt, denial, depression, and sadness. We might also feel a sense of relief if we're helping end the pain of a pet that might be suffering for whatever reason. If you're someone who accepts life and death in a more clinical fashion, it might only take you a matter of weeks to accept the reality of the death, and for others, the process can take years, if ever, to completely get over.

Typically grief will be cyclical – coming in waves or in a series of highs and lows. The lows tend to be deeper and more profound in the beginning and then they gradually become shorter and less painful as time goes by. Grief can also be triggered years after a loss by certain events or stimuli that spark a memory such as a special anniversary, a holiday, seeing an animal that looks similar to the pet that died, a TV show or commercial, a song, a movie, social venues such as Facebook, or a particular sight or sound.

The circumstances of the death will also play a significant role in the stages and duration of grief. If a pet is lost to a sudden and unexpected death there may be more feelings of anger, denial, and sadness. Pet guardians will replay the death over and over – perhaps blaming themselves that they caused the death or that they didn't do enough to save the pet, or there might be anger or blame placed on a veterinarian who was unable to prolong the life of a pet. Grief that stems from these circumstances can be extremely profound, and many will bottle up their feelings to avoid the pain. This is not unusual, but for real healing to happen, at some point the pain will have to be dealt with – ignoring it, misdirecting it, or remaining in denial will only make it worse in the long run.

For some people, finances can factor into the care of a pet, which also can cause feelings of anger, guilt, and despair if they feel they couldn't do everything possible for their pet. Feeling lost or isolated and detached from reality can also occur, and many of us will feel as if our grief is so unbearable that we question if we will be ever be able to move on and function productively in life again.

There might also be displaced anger if you have other pets – maybe you don't understand why one pet died and another didn't. While this is normal, it can cause an enormous sense of guilt and shame for having those feelings of possibly loving one pet more than another. The bottom line is sometimes we have feelings we are ashamed of – but the truth is we are only human – let the range of emotions you're feeling run their course and be patient with yourself.

And while no loss is easy, some deaths are easier to reconcile and the grieving is less severe, such as if a pet has lived a long and happy life and dies peacefully of natural causes. This might also be true if a pet was terminally ill – death might be a relief from the emotional duress that can occur when administering medical care for a prolonged period of time for a pet no longer living a life of quality. In an instance like that, often a pet guardian will make the decision that euthanizing the pet is far more humane than letting it suffer needlessly for an extended period of time. While still difficult, a death like this can give a certain amount of closure because the guardian is typically able to say goodbye to the pet and let them know how much they loved them which lessens the feelings of grief.

Making the ultimate decision to euthanize a pet is not always an easy one however and sometimes a pet guardian will need advice. The process can be extremely confusing and emotionally taxing and in cases like that, it is recommended one rationally evaluate the quality of life the pet is experiencing. Alice Villalobos, DVM, FNAP has a very easy to use Quality of Life Scale that can be found at www.pawspice.com under the resources tab to help guardians decide when or if it is time to provide the gift of a peaceful and painless passing for their pet.

Age is another factor in the grieving process – both our age and the age of the pet that has died. This is especially true if it is a child who is experiencing the loss of a pet for the first time. How they are taught to cope with the grief and pain that accompanies the loss can lay the groundwork – whether positive or negative – on that child's personal development moving forward. It is best to be as gentle and honest as possible about the death for the age appropriateness of the child.

While it might seem kinder on the surface to shield a child from feelings of sadness by either not talking about the pet's death or by pretending the animal ran away or "went to sleep," those scenarios can leave a child feeling angry, confused, or frightened – especially if they think that you, their parent(s), are going to die when you go to sleep at night and abandon them, too.

The best course would be to involve the child in the grieving process as much possible – let them see you grieve and let them know it's okay to feel sad and to miss their pet, too. Rituals and mementos can be important in this regard – let them create a special picture or poem for the pet and hold a memorial service if it seems appropriate. Something like planting a tree in a pet's honor is also therapeutic, but most important of all, reassure the child they weren't responsible for the pet's death and give them time to grieve and heal.

The same holds true regardless of any age – rituals can be very helpful on the road to emotional recovery and we need to have an outlet to say goodbye to our pet and to tell them how much we love them. Whether you believe a pet that passes is given angel wings and finds an afterlife at the Rainbow Bridge where you will meet again one day or you don't, closure, tribute, and paying respect to the pet that has died is important. For example, if the decision is made to have a pet buried, doing something like burying your pet with a favorite blanket or toy or a specially written love note to them can provide a sense of meaning and relief. If a pet is cremated, decorating the urn with pictures and whatnot can also provide emotional relief.

But regardless of any of the circumstances, the most important thing is to let the healing process run its course and to try to be kind to yourself in the meantime. This advice is often the hardest to follow as sometimes we punish ourselves by feeling that if we smile or allow ourselves any happiness we are betraying the memory of the pet we lost. We remain in a dangerous state of denial, blocking out the pain rather than actively dealing with it, which can actually prolong the grieving process in the long run.

All we can do is understand we are human and our feelings of grief are normal and natural. But not everyone will understand that, which is also part of the grieving process. Some people in your life – even close family members or friends – might discount the loss of a pet as being trivial or not on the same level as the loss of a human. Try your best not to take those feelings to heart, and don't let anyone tell you how you should feel or how you should grieve. Your grief is your own and no one else can tell you how or when to get over it or when it's time to move on. Don't ever feel embarrassed to grieve and if you want to cry, scream, or yell, then do it. You and your pet shared a bond that was important to you and no one can take that away from you.

The bottom line – you are not alone. Millions of people across the world can relate to what you're going through – every single person will be completely unique and you might not have the same skin color, speak the same language, be the same sex, or share any other multitude of circumstances and situations, but the one thing in common each and every one of them has with you is that they have also experienced the loss of a pet and understand your pain. And believe it or not, sometimes a perfect stranger can be your best resource toward healing – from blogs to websites to chat rooms and forums. Seek them out – these are people who understand the magnitude of your loss and may be able to get you through your own grieving process (for a full library of these resources, please visit the Association for Pet Loss and Bereavement at www.aplb.org). Numerous books on grieving are also available, and if you feel it is necessary, you could see a therapist for counseling.

Do your best, despite how difficult it may be to make sure you eat a healthy diet, get plenty of sleep, and exercise regularly to help release important endorphins that boost your mood. Grieving can be extremely taxing on the body – both physically and mentally – and often we neglect our own personal care. If you have other pets, try your best to maintain your normal routine with them as they can also become distressed by your sorrow and may be grieving the loss of the pet as well. Try not to let yourself completely detach from reality – reach out to friends, go for a walk, volunteer, take a class – anything that will help elevate your outlook on life.

All you can do is be patient and let the grieving process happen – at some point the pain will soften and will be replaced by the memories of the love and time you shared with your pet. You'll look back with a smile and be thankful that for however long or short the time was, this incredible, devoted, and precious being was a part of your life and enriched your days and nights with their individually unique personality, loyalty, devotion, unconditional love, and companionship.

That's how it is with pets – we open our heart and homes to them, but they are with us for a borrowed time. Treasure each and every moment you are blessed to have with them as if it might be your last because life truly is fleeting. As far as getting another pet, that is a personal decision and one that only you can make when and if the time is right. We can never replace a pet we have lost, and we should never try to. In light of the overwhelming number of animals that need a good home, we can only hope that one day we will find we have room in our heart to love another, just like we opened our hearts to the one we lost.

~The memories and paw prints of a beloved pet remain in our heart and soul forever~

Acknowledgements

WRITING THE STORY of Jazz's life and death was bittersweet for me, as it was not a story I had initially thought I would be writing. But just like he left indelible purr prints on my heart, his sweet and gentle ways touched the hearts of many people that came to know him - from my family to cherished friends I made from blogging and social media. As a result of the outpouring of love, compassion, and support you expressed to me as I struggled to come to terms with saying goodbye to him, this book was born and to all of you, I offer my sincere thanks and gratitude for giving me the inner resolve to make it happen.

Of all these people, a special thank you goes out to Laura Walda of the *Da Tabbies O Trout Towne* blog - while she and I have never met, somehow a bond was forged between us that transcended time and miles. Laura was my silent guiding light and as I was writing, I could feel her championing me along the way, especially during those difficult moments where I would find myself overcome with grief reliving Jazz's ending days.

I am eternally grateful to Dan as well. He and Jazz shared a special friendship and he was with me during the thick and thin of it all and I know he misses his buddy as much as I do. I am blessed to have a companion in my life that is so supportive – writing a book while working full time is no easy task and I know it has cut into our "together" time that we used to share and I appreciate his love, understanding, and patience with the process. I also appreciate his beautiful photos that will forever keep Jazz immortalized and I also thank Karen Robinson for her editing efforts that allowed me to keep Jazz in his wise voice as well as my Mom who gave her editing guidance.

And thank you to my boys, Chris and Joe – Jazz loved you both and if it were not for you giving him to me as a Mother's Day gift, he would never been a part of my life. And my beautiful step-daughters, Crystal and Jackie – you have always been my steady cheerleaders and I can't thank you enough for that. A thank you also to Zee, Zoey, Mia, Peanut, Rolz, Kizmet, and Jazmine – you all remain my feline muses and you brighten my day with your endearing ways and companionship. You are the reason I have become a better person and I learn from you each and every day to stop and take the time to appreciate the small moments that life offers us. And Harley, my darling girl, you left this earth far too early but I am grateful for the time we shared and I just know in my heart that you and Jazz are looking down at me, proud that this story came to be.

I also offer sincere thanks to those of you reading this book that have given a pet a safe and loving home. What a wonderful world it would be if one day all animals had a furever home and in that regard, I am especially grateful to those of you, in whatever capacity, that help with rescue efforts. You are all heroes to me and your love, devotion, compassion, and willingness to help animals in need should be commended.

Lastly, a debt of ingratitude to my dear friends, peers, and colleagues who were kind enough to provide me with testimonial for Jazz's story. I respect and admire each and every one of you and am honored to be a part of such a talented group of people. Your dedication to the welfare of pets is beyond compare and your support means the world to me:

Ingrid King, award-winning author of *Buckley's Story: Lessons from a Feline Master Teacher*, and publisher of *The Conscious Cat*; Caren Gittleman, publisher of *Cat Chat With Caren and Cody*; Alice Villalobos, DVM, FNAP, *www.pawspice.com*; Amy Shojai, CABC, author of 30 pet care books and a founder of the Cat Writers' Association; Layla Morgan-Wilde, holistic cat behaviorist and founder of *Cat Wisdom 101*; Angie Bailey, author of *Texts from Mittens* and *Whiskerslist: The Kitty Classifieds;* Robert Hudson, host and founder, *Pet Radio Show.com*; Bernadette E. Kazmarski, award-winning artist and writer, publisher of *The Creative Cat*; Susan Logan-McCracken, co-author of *Cat Calls* and longtime editor of *Cat Fancy* magazine; Charmaine Hammond, best-selling author and professional speaker; Christine Michaels, founder and president of Pawsitively Humane; Bonnie Poirier, pastor at Ministry of St. Francis of Assisi; and Joanne McGonagle, author of *The Tiniest Tiger* and *An Ordinary Toad's Extraordinary Night,* Instructor of Zoology, Miami University's Global Field Master's Program.

And, of course, Steve Dale, CABC, syndicated radio host, and syndicated newspaper columnist (Tribune Content Agency) – your tongue and cheek introductory paragraph for the foreword in which you took credit for my book - I take the comment in the tone it was intended and find it to be the highest of compliments that you would even suggest it in jest. It was a privilege to have your endorsement and I am humbled by all of your body of works.

Thank you one and all.

About the Author

DEBORAH BARNES resides in the tropical paradise of South Florida with her fiancé and feline family of seven. She is the author of the 5-star rated book, *The Chronicles of Zee & Zoey – A Journey of the Extraordinarily Ordinary* staring her charismatic cats as well as the award winning blog, *Zee & Zoey's Cat Chronicles* that continues to cover the everyday journey she shares with her cats along with topics from the humorous behaviors of cats to very serious subjects on pet responsibility. Deborah was awarded 2013 "Writer of the Year" by Friskies Purina on behalf of the Cat Writers' Association and she is also the Secretary of the nonprofit, Pawsitively Humane, Inc. of Miami, Florida, whose mission is to create public awareness and reduce the numbers of animals on the streets and in shelters through an extensive educational campaign.

Contact Deborah Barnes: info@zzppublishing.com
Follow Purr Prints on Facebook: www.facebook.com/purrprintsoftheheart
Visit *Zee & Zoey's Cat Chronicles:* www.zeezoey.com/blog

Made in the USA
Charleston, SC
02 April 2015